HOW TO TEACH MUSIC
TO CHILDREN

A CREATIVE PLAN OF AWAKENING AND
LEADING CHILDREN INTO MUSIC
WITH A GRADED SYSTEM OF
LESSONS AND MATERIAL
ILLUSTRATED

AND A SUPPLEMENT
THE CHILDREN'S OWN BOOK

BY

ELIZABETH NEWMAN

Price $1.50

CARL FISCHER, Inc.
COOPER SQUARE
NEW YORK

01323

Dedicated to that kindler of
" Joy " in life,
Harriet Ayer Seymour

" Go, little book, and wish to all
   Flowers in the garden, meat in the hall,
   A living river by the door,
   A nightingale in the sycamore."— Stevenson.

AUTHOR'S PREFACE

A PLAN OF AWAKENING AND
LEADING CHILDREN INTO MUSIC

Realizing that most prevalent methods of teaching have made music a tiresome drudgery for childhood, I have evolved a way of making it a thing of delight, a creative fairyland where all children love to dwell. This book has grown out of my studies with Mr. Frederick Schlieder, Miss Helen Wilson, Mrs. Harriet Ayer Seymour, and Miss Angela Diller, who led me into this new realm of musical consciousness, and to whom I wish to express my deep gratitude and appreciation. I am particularly grateful to Mrs. Seymour who encouraged me to undertake and to complete this work, and to Mr. Marshall Bartholomew for his assistance in proof-reading.

The lists of music, games and directions for presenting each subject contained in this book, have been tested from beginning to end by actual use with children and wherever the method herein described may appear to differ from traditional procedure, it is because it has been found to be more practical and effective in dealing with children. In no case, however, is any fundamental principle violated, and the whole plan, when systematically and skillfully carried through, prepares the child easily and naturally for advanced and more technical study of Harmony in later years.

ELIZABETH NEWMAN

PUBLISHERS' NOTE

This book has been prepared to meet a definite need in the field of musical education for children. It was undertaken as the result of a large experience in teaching children, and the discovery that most of the available teaching material at present on the market lacks balance in that it moves too rapidly from the very simple to the fairly difficult, compelling the child to make leaps for which he is not prepared.

In this book, step-wise material for every subject in music, with directions for using, has been carefully collected and arranged, so that the child can gradually develop without there being aroused within him any dislike for music, and without his being forced into performance before his interest and desire have been awakened.

If the material of this volume be followed, it will acquaint children with the best musical literature; the songs, stories, classics and folk-lore of various nations will awaken them to an inner sense of hearing and a consciousness of rhythm. The growth is guarded and gradual and is attained by singing and by using material especially adapted for each step. By means of rhythmic play, such as singing, clapping, dancing-games and songs with dramatic action, children gradually become interested and are thus led through every step of musical development. The result achieved will be a real understanding of the fundamentals which are the bases of all musical development.

The topical outlines are not intended as fixed ones for teachers to follow, but as practical and suggestive helps. In order that teachers may express their own individuality, other songs and ideas may be used, provided they work toward the same goal.

Blank pages are added at the end of some chapters to give space for the original games and additional lists of songs that the student of this work may desire to include.

The supplement "THE CHILDREN'S OWN BOOK" published separately in regular music form with notes of ample size for children to read, contains well selected material carefully graded according to the principles of instruction involved. Phrasing is given as needed, also numerals indicating chords for accompanying harmony.

CONTENTS

LISTS OF BOOKS FOR TEACHERS*

A list of books from which most of the material in this book has been obtained and which contains sufficient material for the purpose of carrying out the directions to teachers.

PIANO

BURCHENAL, E. AND CRAMPTON, C. W. (Compilers). Folk-dance Music, *G. Schirmer, Inc., N. Y.*

HOFER, MARIE RUEF (Compiler). Music for the Child-World, Vol. II (Rhythms, Marches and Games), *Clayton F. Summy Co., Chicago.*

SONGS

HOFER, MARY RUEF (Compiler). Children's Singing Games, Old and New, *Flanagan Co., Chicago, Ill.*

MOFFAT, ALFRED (Compiler). Little Songs of Long Ago, *David McKay, Philadelphia* and *Augener, London.*

NEIDLINGER, W. H. Small Songs for Small Singers, *G. Schirmer, Inc., New York.*

NEWMAN, ELIZABETH (Compiler). The Children's Own Book. *Carl Fischer, Inc., New York.*

PEDERSEN, D. AND BOYD, N. L. (Compilers). Folk Games of Denmark and Sweden, *Saul Bros., Chicago.*

RILEY AND GAYNOR. Songs of the Child World, Vol. I, *John Church Co., Cincinnati, O.*

SURETTE, T. W. AND DAVISON, A. T. (Compilers). Rote Songs for Grades I, II and III, *Boston Music Co.*

A list of other interesting material which may be used and from which some of the material in this book has been obtained. Those marked with a (*) indicate the books from which folk-song material has been taken for this book.

SONGS AND PIANO

CHEATHAM, KITTY (Compiler). Nursery Garland, *G. Schirmer, Inc., New York.*

*NEAL, MARY (Compiler). Esperance Morris Book, Part I, *Curwen & Sons, London.*

*Progressive Music Series. Teachers' Manual, Vols. I, II, III and IV, *Silver, Burdette Co., Boston.*

* Any of the books referred to in this volume may be procured at the Seymour School of Musical Re-Education, 57 West 48th Street, New York City, and at Carl Fischer, Inc., 56–62 Cooper Square, New York City, and at their branch stores in Boston and Chicago.

PIANO

*CRAWFORD, CAROLYN, Dramatic Games and Dances for Little Children, *A. S. Barnes Co., New York.*

*PRAHL, E. V. (Compiler). A First, Second and Third Piano Book — Old Tunes for Young Pianists, *Carl Fischer, Inc., New York.*

*IDE, C. E. AND SEYMOUR, H. A. (Compilers). Seven and Sixty Folk-Songs, *G. Schirmer, Inc., New York.*

SONGS

Appleton Green Series — One Hundred Songs that Children Love to Sing, *D. Appleton, New York.*

COOLIDGE, ELIZABETH. After Supper Songs, *G. Schirmer, Inc., New York.*

Cradle Songs of all Nations. *Clayton F. Summy Co., Chicago.*

DUNNING, SARA L. (Compiler). Fifty-five Rounds and Canons, *G. Schirmer, Inc., New York.*

ELLIOT, J. W. Mother Goose's Nursery Rhymes and Nursery Songs, *McLoughlin Bros., Springfield, Mass.*

FARNSWORTH, C. H. AND SHARP, C. J. (Editors). Folk Songs, Chanteys and Singing Games, *H. W. Gray Co., New York.*

*GOMME, A. B. AND SHARP, C. J. (Editors). Children's Singing Games, Sets I to V, *Novello & Co., London.*

KORBAY, E. Hungarian Melodies, Books I and II, *Schott & Co., G. Schirmer, Inc., New York.*

Russian Folk Songs No. 565. *G. Schirmer, Inc., New York.* (Litolf Edition.)

ROBERT COVERLY. Little Songs for Little Folks, *White-Smith Music Publishing Co., Boston.*

*Morning Stars Sang Together. (Folk-Songs and other Songs for Children.) *Oliver Ditson Co., Boston.*

*Most Popular Mother Goose Songs. *Hinds, Noble and Eldredge, New York.*

OLDS, W. B. Twenty-five Bird Songs for Children, *G. Schirmer, Inc., New York.*

*PEDERSON, D. AND BOYD, N. L. (Compilers). Folk Games and Gymnastic Play, *Saul Bros., Chicago.*

REINECKE, CARL. Fifty Songs, *G. Schirmer, Inc., New York.*

SMITH, ELEANOR. Book of Songs, *Milton Bradley Co., New York.*

*SHARP, CECIL J. (Editor). Collection of Folk-Songs, *Oliver Ditson Co., Boston.*

SHARP, CECIL J. (Editor). English Folk Chanteys, *H. W. Gray & Co., New York.*

*Songs the Whole World Sings. *D. Appleton & Co., New York.*

*SPAECK, A. AND BOYD, N. L. (Editors). Folk Dances of Bohemia and Moravia, *Saul Bros., Chicago.*

*WIDOR, C. M. (Compiler). Vieilles Chansons et Rondes, *Nourritt & Co., Paris.*

The following books provide for the teacher, a background of greater understanding of *Child Psychology.*

DEWEY, JOHN. Democracy of Education, *The Macmillan Co., New York.*
DEWEY, JOHN AND E. R. Schools of Tomorrow, *E. P. Dutton Co., New York.*
HENDERSON, CHAS. HANFORD. Education and the Larger Life, What is it to be Educated? *Houghton, Mifflin, Boston.*
HOLMES, EDMOND (Gore Alexander). Tragedy of Education, *Constable & Co., London.*
HOLMES, EDMOND. What is and what might be, *E. P. Dutton, New York.*
JAMES, WILLIAM. Pragmatism, *Longmans, Green & Co., New York.*
JAMES, WILLIAM. Talks to Teachers on Psychology, *Holt, N. Y.*
KIRKPATRICK, EDWIN A. Fundamentals of Child Study, *The Macmillan Co.*
LELAND, CHARLES GODFREY. The Mystic Will, *Progress Co., Chicago.*
OPPENHEIM, NATHAN. Development of the Child, *The Macmillan Co., New York.*
SADLER, WM. S. Physiology of Faith and Fear, *A. C. McClurg & Co., Chicago.*
THOMSON, W. HANNA. Brain and Personality, *Dodd, Mead & Co., New York.*
TROWARD, THOMAS. Creative Process of the Individual, *McBride, New York.*
WHITE, WM. A. Principles of Mental Hygiene, *The Macmillan Co., New York.*

ON THE ART AND SCIENCE OF MUSIC

BARTHOLOMEW, M. AND LAWRENCE, R. Music for Everybody, *Abingdon Press, New York.*
BUSONI, F. B. Sketch of a New Esthetic in Music, *G. Schirmer, New York.*
CADY, CALVIN B. Music Education, *Clayton F. Summy Co., Chicago.*
CADY, CALVIN B. Music Education, Book II, *Clayton F. Summy Co., Chicago.*
DAVIES, F. D. Singing of the Future, *John Lane, London.*
GLYN, MARGARET. Analysis of the Evolution of Musical Form, *Longmans, Green & Co., London.*
GLYN, MARGARET. Rhythmic Conception of Music, *Longmans, Green & Co., London.*
HELMHOLTZ. On the Sensation of Tone as a Physiological Basis for the Theory of Music, *Green & Co., New York.*
JACQUES-DALCROZE, EMILE. Eurythmics, *Small, Maynard Co., Boston.*
MACPHERSON, STEWART. Musical Education of the Child, *Boston Music Co.*
PATTERSON, CHAS. BRODIE. Rhythm of Life, *Crowell Co., New York.*
SCHAUFFLER, ROBERT HAVEN. Musical Amateur, *Houghton, Mifflin, Boston.*
SEYMOUR, HARRIET A. How to Think Music, *G. Schirmer, New York.*
SEYMOUR, HARRIET A. What Music Can Do For You, *Harper, New York.*
SURETTE, THOS. WHITNEY. Music and Life, *Houghton, Mifflin, Boston.*
TROTTER, THOS. HENRY YORKE. Making of Musicians, *E. P. Dutton & Co., New York.*
WOODHOUSE, GEORGE. Artist at the Piano, *Charles Scribner, New York.*

HOW TO TEACH MUSIC TO CHILDREN

CHAPTER I

CLASS AND TEACHER

As environment is most suggestive for successful work, a bright and attractive room should be chosen for the class lessons, flowers and appropriate pictures used, and the entire place filled with an atmosphere of cheerfulness and harmony. The necessary equipment should consist of a piano, a blackboard and small chairs.

For the best work, the class should be limited to six children, as nearly as possible of the same age. Under ordinary conditions, about two lessons a week of forty-five minutes each are given to the class; but a more ideal plan of school management provides a half hour period for the music lesson each school day. However, even the plan of giving two lessons a week of forty-five minutes each, gives very young beginners sufficient " practise-time " in class, until the growing interest and ability of the child produce the enthusiasm and desire to go to the keyboard and work and play there of his own volition. A private lesson once a week is added to the class lessons after a child has attained a sufficient musical realization to be able to hear a tune which includes all of the tones of the scale and its harmony.

As it is essential to preserve animated interest throughout a class lesson, a frequent change of subject is advisable. This change and arrangement of program depend upon the mood of the children and upon the subjects that are to be considered at a particular time. The subjects evolved in this work are not intended to be given successively, but in each class lesson a change should be made about every five minutes. The suggested program which follows in this chapter should also undergo a similar variation until all the subject matter contained in each chapter has been brought into use in the order given.

1

The first three subjects to be introduced and continued in every class lesson are — *Rhythm, Creative Work* and the *Musical Story Period.* Simultaneously with them and successively (since there would not be sufficient time for all of the remaining subjects in every class lesson) the *Home-tone, Scale* and *Melody* should be given. *Harmony, Notation* and *The First Songs for the Children to Play* (Chapter XI) may be introduced after about two or three months of class work. The programs arranged in this manner would include all of the subject matter intended to be given within a period of one or two weeks. In this way the children are given sufficient practice and knowledge of each subject to enable them to express themselves correctly when they are ready to go to the keyboard. Herewith is given an illustration of one class lesson as a suggestion to the teacher.

1. **Songs.**
2. **Creative expression.**
3. **Rhythmical expression — as marching, skipping, running, etc.**
4. **Melody.**
5. **Game for Rhythm.**
6. **Scale Song.**
7. **Song for Dramatic expression.**
8. **Home tone.**
9. **Story and Music.**

For successful results in this work, it is necessary for the teacher to keep the vision constantly before her of the ultimate goal to be reached, and to guide the children logically and continuously through every progressive step, from the simple to the complex, without omitting any of the important links. To do this requires versatility, adaptability and imagination. New possibilities will constantly unfold for the teacher, as they do for the children, because music, like life, is always in the making, never completed. Perhaps a better word than teacher would be " Guide "; one who leads the children on a journey of exploration, as it were, and, with hints here and suggestions there, enables them to make their own discoveries of every new principle introduced.

If the directions in this book should at times appear dogmatic, or fixed, or too explanatory, it is with the intention only of making them very clear and definite.

The folk-songs listed in Chapter XI and appearing in "The Children's Own Book," are intended to be the first musical selections expressed by the children at the keyboard.

CHAPTER II

RHYTHM

"The world began in motion and number." — PYTHAGORAS.

"Musical training is a more potent instrument than any other, because rhythm and harmony find their way into the secret places of the soul on which they mightily fasten, imparting grace and making the soul graceful of him who is rightly educated." — PLATO.

As the movement of life itself in the universe is rhythmic, so rhythm is the very life and soul of music. This movement is felt rather than known, and if not consciously felt by each individual, can nearly always be awakened and developed.

The sense of rhythm belongs to the subconscious powers and is not attained by pure intellection. It is inherent in every child, and music is a natural means of awakening the rhythmic sense.

The First Expression of Rhythm

The first expression of rhythm is given by means of songs for dramatic action, and games to which the children react as the music or words suggest. They use their own initiative. They sway back and forth, or they march while playing imaginary instruments. Or they run, skip, dance, clap and gallop to match the music with satisfying motion. The appended lists of songs suggest the action to be followed.

List of Songs for Dramatic Action

Children are born actors; their interest is maintained as long as their imagination is fired. The following songs suggest some form of dramatic action which the children themselves can devise while singing; this develops freedom, originality and rhythm.

FOR DRAMATIC ACTION

How Many Miles to Boston Town?
  NEWMAN, *The Children's Own Book*, p. 24.
Dancing Fairies:
  NEWMAN, *The Children's Own Book*, p. 7.
I Had a Little Nut Tree:
  NEWMAN, *The Children's Own Book*, p. 16.
Mr. Frog:
  NEIDLINGER, *Small Songs for Small Singers*, p. 28.
Mr. Duck and Mr. Turkey:
  NEIDLINGER, *Small Songs for Small Singers*, p. 32.
Pretty Little Blue Bird:
  NEIDLINGER, *Small Songs for Small Singers*, p. 30.
Little Shoemaker:
  RILEY AND GAYNOR, *Songs of the Child World*, p. 17.
Apple Tree House:
  SURETTE, *Rote Songs*, p. 35.
Planting a Garden:
  SURETTE, *Rote Songs*, p. 35.
The Blacksmith:
  RILEY AND GAYNOR, *Songs of the Child World*, p. 16.
Rhythm Game:
  RILEY AND GAYNOR, *Songs of the Child World*, p. 108.
Eskimo Hunter:
  (Eskimo Folk-song), *Progressive Music Series, Teachers' Manual*, Vol. I,
    p. 220.
Elves and the Shoemaker:
  Progressive Music Studies, Teachers' Manual, Vol. I, p. 252.
Cock Robin:
  Progressive Music Studies, Teachers' Manual, Vol. II, p. 176.
The Brass-band:
  Progressive Music Studies, Teachers' Manual, Vol. II, p. 264.
Nursery Rhymes:
Over the Hills and Far Away (one child pipes Tom's song):
  MOFFAT, *Little Songs of Long Ago*, p. 11.
Little Jumping Joan:
  NEWMAN, *The Children's Own Book*, p. 26.
Lavender's Blue:
  NEWMAN, *The Children's Own Book*, p. 14.

CLAPPING AND STAMPING

Bohemian — With both my hands I Clap, Clap, Clap:
  Folk-games and Gymnastic Play, p. 12.
The Hopping Dance — *Folk-games of Bohemia and Moravia*, p. 27.

Danish — Clap, Clap, Courtesy:
> Burchenal and Crampton, *Folk-dances*, p. 3.

English — Shoemaker's Dance:
> Burchenal and Crampton, *Folk-dances*, p. 10.

French — Polka for Clapping:
> *Vieilles Chansons*, p. 47.

German — Hopping Dance:
> Hofer, *Music for the Child World*, Vol. II, p. 83.

German — Little Playmate Dance with Me:
> Hofer, *Children's Singing Games*, p. 7.

Heel and Toe:
> *Folk-games and Gymnastic Play*, p. 18.

Scotch — Chimes of Dunkirk:
> Hofer, *Music for the Child World*, Vol. II, p. 83.

Swedish — In Wooden Shoes:
> *Progressive Music Series, Teacher's Manual*, Vol. I, p. 214.

Swedish — Clap Dance:
> *Folk-games of Denmark and Sweden*, p. 26.

Clapping Song:
> Riley and Gaynor, *Songs of the Child World*, p. 119.

MARCHING

Piano

Aida — March from, Verdi.

Tannhauser — March from, Wagner.

Faust — March from, Gounod.

March Militaire — Concone:
> Hofer, *Music for the Child World*, Vol. II, p. 36.

Norwegian Mountain March:
> Burchenal and Crampton, *Folk-dances*, p. 25.

Soldiers' March:
> Schumann, *Album for the Young*.

SONGS FOR MARCHING

We March Like Soldiers:
> Riley and Gaynor, *Songs of the Child World*, p. 34.

Rub-a-dub-dub:
> Riley and Gaynor, *Songs of the Child World*, p. 32.

Marching Song:
> Riley and Gaynor, *Songs of the Child World*, p. 32.

Lead Soldiers:
> *Folk-games and Gymnastic Play*, p. 201.

Our Flag:
> Neidlinger, *Small Songs for Small Singers*, p. 34.

Tin Soldiers:
> Neidlinger, *Small Songs for Small Singers*, p. 31.

FRENCH

Papa — Les Petits Bateaux, *Vieilles Chansons*, p. 30.

WALKING

Walk Like Fairies:
> HOFER, *Music for the Child World*, Vol. II, p. 6.

This is the Way My Dolly Walks:
> CRAWFORD, *Dramatic Games and Dances*, p. 3.

Follow My Leader:
> CRAWFORD, *Dramatic Games and Dances*, p. 3.

The Little Ducks:
> CRAWFORD, *Dramatic Games and Dances*, p. 15.

Visiting Game:
> HOFER, *Children's Singing Games*, p. 31.

Walking Tune — Old Irish Tune:
> PRAHL, *Comp. Old Tunes for Young Pianists*, Vol. III, p. 19.

RUNNING

Fisher's Hornpipe:
> BURCHENAL AND CRAMPTON, *Folk Dances*, p. 16.

Game of Tag:
> HOFER, *Music for the Child World*, p. 14.

Hornpipe:
> BURCHENAL AND CRAMPTON, *Folk Dances*, p. 11.

Lazy Sheep, Pray Tell Me Why:
> SURETTE, *Rote Songs*, p. 4.

Run, Run, Run:
> HOFER, *Music for the Child World*, Vol. II, p. 3.

GALLOPING

(Trotting, Cantering, Ambling or High Stepping)

PIANO

Hunting Song — SCHUMANN.

Wild Rider — SCHUMANN.

Gallop from William Tell: ROSSINI,
> GOENSCHEL, *Duet Book for Children*, Vol. II.

SONGS

Hop, hop, hop:
> NEWMAN, *The Children's Own Book*, p. 10.

Pony Ride:
> SURETTE, *Rote Songs*, p. 12.

Riding on a Crow:
> *Folk Games of Denmark and Sweden*, p. 49.

Oh, A-Hunting We Will Go:
> GOMME AND SHARP, *Children's Singing Games*, Set II, p. 14.

Here We Come Gathering Nuts in May:
GOMME AND SHARP, *Children's Singing Games.*

SKIPPING

PIANO

Country Dance — English:
BURCHENAL AND CRAMPTON, *Folk Dance Music*, p. 16.
Highland Fling — Scotch:
BURCHENAL AND CRAMPTON, *Folk Dance Music*, p. 29.
Hippity Hop:
NEWMAN, *The Children's Own Book*, p. 25.
Garry Owen — Irish:
HOFER, *Music for the Child World*, Vol. II, p. 126.
Irish Washerwoman:
BURCHENAL AND CRAMPTON, *Folk Dance Music*, p. 22.
St. Patrick's Day:
BURCHENAL AND CRAMPTON, *Folk Dance Music*, p. 33.
Sicilienne:
SCHUMANN, *Album for the Young.*
Tarantelle — Italian:
BURCHENAL AND CRAMPTON, *Folk-dance Music*, p. 24.
Sicilienne: MULLER:
PRAHL, *Old Tunes For Young Pianists*, Vol. III, p. 5.
Duke of Marlborough:
BURCHENAL AND CRAMPTON, *Folk-Dance Music*, p. 6.

SONGS

Gold and Crimson Tulips:
RILEY AND GAYNOR, *Songs of the Child World*, p. 82.
Robin-a-Thrush:
SURETTE, *Rote Songs*, p. 33.
Sleighing Song:
RILEY AND GAYNOR, *Songs of the Child World*, p. 70.

FOR DANCING

PIANO

BRAHMS — Waltz in A♭.
CHOPIN — Prelude in A:
(With words in CHEATHAM, *Nursery Garland*, p. 143)
CHOPIN — Waltz in C:
(With words in CHEATHAM, *Nursery Garland*, p. 24.)
CHOPIN — Waltz in G♭.
GOUNOD — Waltz from Faust.
GRIEG — Elfin Dance:
(With words in CHEATHAM, *Nursery Garland*, p. 26.)

GRIEG — Waltz in Albumleaf, G minor.
MOZART — From Magic Flute, Elfin Invitation:
    CHEATHAM, *Nursery Garland*, p. 8.
STRAUSS — Blue Danube Waltz:
    (With words in CHEATHAM, *Nursery Garland*, p. 20.)
VON WEBER — Waltz from Der Freischütz:
    HOFER, *Music for the Child World*, Vol. II, 130.

SONGS

A Walk in the Woods — (Walking and Dancing):
    Folk Games of Denmark and Sweden, p. 48.
Come Let Us Be Dancing:
    NEWMAN, *The Children's Own Book*.
Dance of the Rainbow Fairies:
    RILEY AND GAYNOR, *Songs of the Child World*, p. 54.
Dancing and Turning:
    Folk Games of Bohemia and Moravia, p. 18.
Dancing Game:
    RILEY AND GAYNOR, *Songs of the Child World*, p. 101.
Girl is Walking in the Ring:
    (Swedish) *Folk Games of Denmark and Sweden*, p. 21.
Handerchief Dance:
    Folk Games of Bohemia and Moravia, p. 26.
Lady Slipper:
    Folk Games of Bohemia and Moravia, p. 31.
Two Knights — (For walking and dancing):
    Folk Games of Denmark and Sweden, p. 44.
Nous N'irons Plus au Bois:
    Vieilles Chansons, p. 26.

MINUETS

BACH — Minuet in G.
BEETHOVEN — Minuet in G.
GRIEG — Grandmother's Minuet:
    (With words in CHEATHAM, *Nursery Garland*, p. 22.)
MOZART — Minuet in F:
    HOFER, *Music for the Child World*, Vol. II, p. 82.
MOZART — Minuet (Written at the age of four):
    (With words in CHEATHAM, *Nursery Garland*, p. 11.)
MOZART — The Minuet (With words):
    Progressive Music Series, Teacher's Manual, Vol. III, p. 195.

GAVOTTES

GHYS — Air du Roi Louis XIII:
    HOFER, *Music for the Child's World*, Vol. II, p. 129.
GLUCK — Gavotte:
    CHEATHAM, *Nursery Garland*, p. 14.

Singing Folk-Games

These may also be used for teaching Pitch and Harmony and "For First Songs to be Played." (The following games are harmonized with only the I, V and V_7 chords.)

Duke and the Castle:
    HOFER, *Children's Singing Games*, p. 10.
Looby Loo:
    NEWMAN, *Children's Own Book*, p. 11.
King of France:
    HOFER, *Children's Singing Games*, p. 8.
London Bridge:
    HOFER, *Children's Singing Games*, p. 13.
Oats, Peas, Beans:
    HOFER, *Children's Singing Games*, p. 22.
Here Comes One Soldier Marching:
    HOFER, *Children's Singing Games*, p. 9.
The Farmer in the Dell:
    HOFER, *Children's Singing Games*, p. 20.
Here We Go Round the Mulberry Bush:
    HOFER, *Children's Singing Games*, p. 18.
Mulberry Bush:
    Progressive Series, Teacher's Manual, Vol. I, p. 199.
Jolly is the Miller:
    HOFER, *Children's Singing Games*, p. 23.
Hunt the Slipper:
    HOFER, *Children's Singing Games*, p. 19.
Musician:]
    HOFER, *Children's Singing Games*, p. 28.
Thorn Rosa:
    Folk Games of Denmark and Sweden, p. 32.
Will You Know:
    Folk Games and Gymnastic Play, p. 35.
The Haying Party:
    Folk Games and Gymnastic Play, p. 17.
The Washing Game:
    Folk Games of Denmark and Sweden, p. 46.
Wigamy, Wigamy, Water-hen:
    NEAL, *Espérance Morris*, Book I, p. 47.
Nuts in May:
    CRAWFORD, *Dramatic Games and Dances*, p. 37.
Away We All Go:
    CRAWFORD, *Dramatic Games and Dances*, p. 5.

Green Gravel:
    CHEATHAM, *Nursery Garland*, p. 84.

LIST OF GAMES IN WHICH THE I, IV, V AND V₇ CHORDS ARE USED

The Muffin Man:
    HOFER, *Children's Singing Games*, p. 19.
Round and Round the Village:
    NEWMAN, *The Children's Own Book*, p. 16.
Annie Goes to the Cabbage Field:
    HOFER, *Children's Singing Games*, p. 39.
Comin' Thro' the Rye:
    HOFER, *Children's Singing Games*, p. 41.
Dame Get Up and Bake Your Pies (Minor):
    NEWMAN, *The Children's Own Book*, p. 34.
While Traveling Over Land and Sea:
    Folk Games and Gymnastic Play, p. 34.
The Dog and the Hare:
    Folk Games and Gymnastic Play, p. 14.
Lady Fair:
    HOFER, *Children's Singing Games*, p. 27.

GAMES IN WHICH THE I, II, V AND V₇ CHORDS ARE USED

Green Grass:
    NEAL, *Espérance Morris*, Book I, p. 54.
O! A-hunting We Will Go:
    GOMME AND SHARPE (Editors), *Children's Singing Games*, Set II, p. 14.
Old Roger's Dead:
    NEAL, *Espérance Morris*, Book I, p. 48.
Shepherdess:
    HOFER, *Children's Singing Games*, p. 25.
Harvest Game — Will You Know How the Farmer?
    Folk Games of Denmark and Sweden, p. 52.
Three Dukes:
    GOMME AND SHARP, *Children's Singing Games*, Set I, p. 20.
How Many Miles to Boston Town?
    NEWMAN, *The Children's Own Book*, p. 24.
Jennie Jones:
    GOMME AND SHARP (Editors), *Children's Singing Games*, Set III, p. 2.

OTHERS OF MORE DIFFICULT HARMONIZATION

Little Playmates:
    HOFER, *Children's Singing Games*, p. 31.
Hänsel and Gretel Dance:
    HOFER, *Children's Singing Games*, p. 40.
The Thread Follows the Needle:
    CRAWFORD, *Dramatic Games and Dances*, p. 7.

Punchinello:
>HOFER, *Children's Singing Games*, p. 29.

Indian Song (To be used as a Game):
>*Progressive Music Series, Teacher's Manual*, Vol. I, p. 136.

O, When I was a Schoolgirl:
>GOMME AND SHARP (Editors), *Children's Singing Games*, Set II, p. 10.

FRENCH AND ENGLISH GAMES

Garden Game— This is How We Spade the Ground:
>HOFER, *Children's Singing Games*, p. 21.

Savez-vous Planter les Choux?
>NEWMAN, *The Children's Own Book*, p. 9.

Have You Seen the Soldiers?
>HOFER, *Children's Singing Games*, p. 12.

As-tu vu la Casquette?
>NEWMAN, *The Children's Own Book*, p. 12.

In the Land of France:
>HOFER, *Children's Singing Games*, p. 36.

La Monaco:
>*Vieilles Chansons*, p. 31.

Le Pont D'Avignon:
>NEWMAN, *The Children's Own Book*, p. 12.

Musician:
>HOFER, *Children's Singing Games*, p. 28.

La Mist en Laire:
>*Vieilles Chansons*, p. 10.

Punchinello:
>HOFER, *Children's Singing Games*, p. 29.

La Polichinelle:
>*Vieilles Chansons*, p. 8.

GAME FOR TAPPING THE TIME
(Created by Marjorie Dice)

The picture of a snow-man is drawn on the board and as the teacher plays a selection of simple and well-marked rhythm, the children illustrate a snowstorm by tapping the time as they draw the snowflakes. Again, when a chord is played by the teacher, they draw a picture of a snowball.

ANOTHER FORM OF THE SAME GAME: TO REPRESENT A
SUMMER SHOWER

Flowers are drawn on the board, and, as the teacher plays, the children tap the raindrops to the time of the music. When a chord is played, they draw a picture of the sun.

A Rhythmic Game

FOR TEACHERS' NOTES

CHAPTER III
RHYTHM (Continued)

The word " Rhythm " is derived from a Greek term meaning
" to flow "; and it is this flowing movement — this moving force
of Life itself — that the child is led to feel. But as Rhythm includes *Time, Phrasing, Pattern or Design,* and *Form,* this subject
can be given to children part by part only; and not until each part
is thoroughly *felt* can the child grasp and assemble in *feeling* the
symmetry and balance of the whole.

So the children are first led to feel the swing of each measure in
the *Lullabies* and *Other Songs;* then the *Swing* and *Time* in the
folk-songs, folk-dances and holiday songs, and then the *Swing,
Time, Phrasing, Pattern* and *Form* in the songs listed in Chapter
XI, " First Songs for the Children to Play," and contained in
" The Children's Own Book."

Folk-songs are used because they are the most valuable material
we have for beginners.   Such songs are the result of natural feeling
and express the primitive emotions in which the great law of
rhythm never fails.   It is for this reason they have been chosen as
standards for Rhythm and Form by our greatest composers in
countless Sonatas, Symphonies, and various other compositions.

(a) Directions for Swinging by Means of Lullabies and Other Songs

As the teacher plays from the following list of songs, the children
are quiet and listen in order to be able to swing when they feel the
rhythm.   When this is felt, they give each measure a swing. If
they are unable to feel this, the teacher asks them to tell of something they have seen or felt that moves rhythmically.   Such
answers have been given as, the flying of a bird, the swimming of
a fish, the running of a rabbit, and the beating of the heart.
Helpful illustrations for the teacher to use are the rocking of a
cradle and the swinging of the pendulum.

In these illustrations the child is lead to feel that the change of each swing necessitates some force to move it in the opposite direction, and that the same force is to be felt when their own swing changes for each measure.

The teacher also leads the children to a realization that their personal lives can express the same beauty that is found in music; that whatever they express in art is really an expression of themselves, and that in order to keep this expression beautiful and harmonious they must be constantly on guard to make their thoughts and lives rhythmical, healthy and joyous. She should seek to inspire such *faith* that fear can find no place.

LISTS FOR SWINGING

Lullabies and Songs

2/4 Cradle Song:
   NEWMAN, *The Children's Own Book*, p. 15.
   Slumber Song:
   SURETTE, *Rote Songs*, p. 53.
3/8 Lullaby — Indian Melody from Hiawatha:
   CRAWFORD, *Dramatic Games and Dances*, p. 53.
3/4 Rosebush's Baby:
   NEIDLINGER, *Small Songs for Small Singers*, p. 2.
   Love's Lullaby:
   CHEATHAM, *Nursery Garland*, p. 146.
   Cradle Song — BRAHMS:
   CHEATHAM, *Nursery Garland*, p. 128.
   Little Birdie:
   NEIDLINGER, *Small Songs for Small Singers*, p. 43.
   Busy Folks — Folk-song:
   Progressive Music Series, Teacher's Manual, Vol. I, p. 221.
4/4 Little Sister's Lullaby — Folk-song:
   Progressive Music Series, Teacher's Manual, Vol. I, p. 206.
   Bye, Baby, Bye:
   NEWMAN, *The Children's Own Book*, p. 4.
   The Little Dustman:
   NEWMAN, *The Children's Own Book*, p. 29.
6/8 Little Land — Mozart (Stevenson):
   CHEATHAM, *Nursery Garland*, p. 125.
   Rock-a-bye, Baby:
   Songs the Whole World Sings, p. 182.

INSTRUMENTAL

Schumann — Lullaby, and other selections from among the well known classics.

OTHER SONGS

2/4 I See You:
Folk Games of Denmark and Sweden, p. 25.
The Robin's Song:
Newman, *The Children's Own Book*, p. 8.
Tulips:
Riley and Gaynor, *Songs of the Child World*, p. 82.
Little Polly Flinders:
Moffat, *Little Songs of Long Ago*, p. 13.
Saw the Lumber:
Folk Games and Gymnastic Plays, p. 29.
Sleighing Song:
Riley and Gaynor, *Songs of the Child World*, p. 70.

3/4 Come Let Us be Dancing:
Newman, *The Children's Own Book*, p. 13.
See-Saw:
Riley and Gaynor, *Songs of the Child World*, p. 97.
Swing Song:
Surette, *Rote Songs*, p. 58.
Reap the Flax:
Folk-games of Denmark and Sweden, p. 38.
Golden Boat:
Surette, *Rote Songs*, p. 26.
Autumn Leaves:
Progressive Music Series, Teacher's Manual, Vol. I, p. 234.

4/4 Bird's Nest:
Riley and Gaynor, *Songs of the Child-World*, p. 10.
River:
Riley and Gaynor, *Songs of the Child World*, p. 48.
My Doggie's Name is Guess:
Riley and Gaynor, *Songs of the Child World*, p. 47.
Old King Cole:
Newman, *The Children's Own Book*, p. 36.
Sing a Song of Six-pence:
Songs the Whole World Sings, p. 196.

6/8 Land of Nod:
Riley and Gaynor, *Songs of the Child World*, p. 11.
Moon-Boat:
Riley and Gaynor, *Songs of the Child World*, p. 61.

Little Jack Horner:
NEWMAN, *The Children's Own Book*, p. 18.
Hey, Diddle, Diddle:
NEWMAN, *The Children's Own Book*, p. 30.

(b) Directions for Discovering the " Time " by Means of Folk-Songs and Dances

1. While the teacher plays with well-marked rhythm and expression, the children listen; then, when they feel the rhythm, they swing with a swing for each measure.

2. Next, the teacher explains that the mathematical side of rhythm consists of a regular number of beats within each swing which they can determine by clapping. The children clap and say " ONE " at the place where the swing changes. If this change, however, is not readily felt, half of the class swing while the others clap.

3. The teacher then asks the children to clap and count softly the beats that come after the " One," and determine for themselves if the same number of them is contained in each swing or measure. If the children are inclined to clap according to long and short tones, one-third of the class is directed to march, one-third to clap the marching steps, and one-third to swing. By this process they readily discover the even number of beats.

LISTS OF SONGS FOR SWINGING AND FOR CLAPPING THE TIME

FOLK-SONGS AND DANCES

American:
  2/4 Dixie Land — *Morning Stars Sang Together*, p. 165.
     Yankee Doodle — NEWMAN, *The Children's Own Book*, p. 23.
  3/4 America — NEWMAN, *The Children's Own Book*, p. 28.
     Star-Spangled Banner — *Morning Stars Sang Together*, p. 160; *Progressive Music Series*, Vol. II, p. 310.
  4/4 Battle Hymn of the Republic — *Songs the Whole World Sings*, p. 233.
Bohemian:
  2/4 Strasak — BURCHENAL AND CRAMPTON, *Folk-dance Music*, p. 2.
     Geese in the Wheatfield — *Folk Dances of Bohemia and Moravia*, p. 21.
     Gingham Apron — *Folk Dances of Bohemia and Moravia*, p. 22.
     Komarno — BURCHENAL AND CRAMPTON, *Folk Dance Music*, p. 3.
     Polka — HOFER, *Music for the Child-World*, Vol. III, p. 130.
  3/4 Handkerchief Dance — *Folk-dances of Bohemia and Moravia*, p. 26.
     Lady Slipper — *Folk-dances of Bohemia and Moravia*, p. 31.

Danish:
    2/4 Dance of Greeting — BURCHENAL AND CRAMPTON, *Folk-dance Music*, p. 4.

English:
    2/4 Chorus Jig — BURCHENAL AND CRAMPTON, *Folk-dance Music*, p. 14.
    The Crested Hen — NEWMAN, *The Children's Own Book*, p. 28.
    English Hornpipe — BURCHENAL AND CRAMPTON, *Folk-dance Music*, p. 11.
    Shoemaker's Dance — BURCHENAL AND CRAMPTON, *Folk-dance Music*, p. 10.
    3/4 Little Man in a Fix — BURCHENAL AND CRAMPTON, *Folk-dance Music*, p. 12.
    4/4 Fisher's Hornpipe — BURCHENAL AND CRAMPTON, *Folk-dance Music*, p. 16.
    Harvest Dance — BURCHENAL AND CRAMPTON, *Folk-dance Music*, p. 17.
    6/8 Country Dance — BURCHENAL AND CRAMPTON, *Folk-dance Music*, p. 16.

National Hymn:
    3/4 God Save the King — *Songs the Whole World Sings*, p. 236.

French:
    2/4 Galop — *Vieilles Chansons*, p. 46.
    Polka — *Vieilles Chansons*, p. 47.

National Hymn:
    4/4 Marseillaise — *Morning Stars Sang Together*, p. 175.

German:
    2/4 German Hopping Dance — HOFER, *Music for the Child-World*, Vol. II, p. 83.
    2/4 German Kinderpolka — BURCHENAL AND CRAMPTON, *Folk-Dance Music*, p. 20.
    3/8 Fir Tree — *Morning Stars Sang Together*, p. 74.
    Lauterbach Song — *Songs the Whole World Sings*, p. 153.
    Lieber Augustin — NEWMAN, *The Children's Own Book*, p. 13.
    6/8 Lorelei — *Morning Stars Sang Together*, p. 76.
    Silent Night — NEWMAN, *The Children's Own Book*, p. 19.

National Hymn:
    4/4 Watch on the Rhine — *Morning Stars Sang Together*, p. 170.

Irish:
    3/8 Cockles and Mussels — *Morning Stars Sang Together*, p. 68.
    3/4 Last Rose of Summer — *Morning Stars Sang Together*, p. 66.
    6/8 Garry Owen — HOFER, *Music for the Child-World*, Vol. II, p. 126.
    Irish Washerwoman — BURCHENAL AND CRAMPTON, *Folk-Dance Music*, p. 22.
    Low-backed Car — *Morning Stars Sang Together*, p. 60.
    St. Patrick's Day — NEWMAN, *The Children's Own Book*, p. 33.

National Song:

2/4 Wearing of the Green — *Songs the Whole World Sings*, p. 238.

Italian:

3/8 Santa Lucia — Neapolitan, *Morning Stars Sang Together*, p. 134.

6/8 Funiculi, Funicula — *Morning Stars Sang Together*, p. 131.

Tarantelle — HOFER, *Music for the Child World*, Vol. II, p. 131.

Tarantelle — BURCHENAL AND CRAMPTON, *Folk-Dance Music*, p. 24.

Norwegian:

4/4 Mountain March — BURCHENAL AND CRAMPTON, *Folk-Dance Music*, p. 25.

Russian:

2/4 Comarinskaia — BURCHENAL AND CRAMPTON, *Folk-Dance Music*, p. 26.

4/4 Russian National Hymn — *Songs the Whole World Sings*, p. 249.

Scotch:

2/4 Auld Lang Syne — *Morning Stars Sang Together*, p. 64.

Chimes of Dunkirk — BURCHENAL AND CRAMPTON, *Folk-Dance Music*, p. 31.

Highland Fling, I — BURCHENAL AND CRAMPTON, *Folk-Dance Music*, p. 29.

Highland Fling, II — BURCHENAL AND CRAMPTON, *Folk-Dance Music*, p. 30.

4/4 Comin' Thro' the Rye — *Morning Stars Sang Together*, p. 40.

Highland Schottische — BURCHENAL AND CRAMPTON, *Folk-Dance Music*, p. 31.

Shean Trews — BURCHENAL AND CRAMPTON, *Folk-Dance Music*, p. 29.

6/8 The Campbells are Comin' (Old Melody, 16th Century) — *Morning Stars Sang Together*, p. 52.

National Song:

4/4 Blue Bells of Scotland — *Songs the Whole World Sings*, p. 248.

Spanish:

2/4 La Paloma (The Dove) — *Morning Stars Sang Together*, p. 156.

3/8 La Cachucha, *Morning Stars Sang Together*, p. 150.

Swedish:

2/4 Hopp, Mor Annika — BURCHENAL AND CRAMPTON, *Folk-Dance Music*, p. 53.

Klapp Dans — BURCHENAL AND CRAMPTON, *Folk-Dance Music*, p. 46.

Lott ist Tod — NEWMAN, *The Children's Own Book*, p. 32.

3/4 Vapperstavels — BURCHENAL AND CRAMPTON, *Folk-Dance Music*, p. 36.

Vinkagersdans — BURCHENAL AND CRAMPTON, *Folk-Dance Music*, p. 36.

SONGS FOR OLDER CHILDREN
(These may also be used for Dramatic Action)

Any of the English folk-songs compiled by Cecil Sharp as:

Raggle Taggle Gypsies:
The Keeper:
Oh, No, John:
Two Magicians:
Tree in the Wood:
or
Rounds:
> SARA L. DUNNING (*Fifty-five Rounds and Canons*).

Any of the folk-songs listed under the subject of Rhythm:

FOLK-DANCES AND SONGS FOR RHYTHM

Tenting on the Old Camp Ground (Three-part song for boys' voices):
> *Progressive Music Series, Teacher's Manual*, Vol. IV, p. 96.
Rowing Song (Three-part song):
> *Progressive Music Series, Teacher's Manual*, Vol. IV, p. 98.
Will You Come With Me?
> *Progressive Music Series, Teacher's Manual*, Vol. I, p. 217.
Hail to Our Class (Four-part song):
> *Progressive Music Series, Teacher's Manual*, Vol. IV, p. 102.
Anvil Chorus — G. Verdi from "Il Trovatore":
> *Progressive Music Series*, Vol. IV, p. 138.

SONGS FOR HOLIDAYS
CHRISTMAS

Christmas Day:
> SURETTE, *Rote Songs*, p. 83.
Christmas Tree Song — (Dance and Song):
> *Folk-games of Denmark and Sweden*, p. 13.
First Noel—Christmas Carol:
> SURETTE, *Rote Songs*, p. 48.
Merry Christmas:
> RILEY AND GAYNOR, *Songs of the Child-World*, p. 27.
Now 'Tis Christmas Time:
> *Folk-games of Denmark and Sweden*, p. 34.
Oh, Christmas Tree — (Sung to the music of Tannenbaum or Pine Tree):
> SURETTE, *Rote Songs*, p. 8.
Oh, Come, All Ye Faithful:
> SURETTE, *Rote Songs*, p. 47.

Old Christmas Carols:
S. ARCHER GIBSON, Sets I to VI, Schirmer Ed.
Santa Claus:
SURETTE, *Rote Songs*, p. 24.
Three Little Kittens:
CHEATHAM, *Nursery Garland*, p. 94.
Three Little Ships — (Game):
CRAWFORD, *Dramatic Games and Dances*, p. 39.

EASTER

Easter Rabbit:
Progressive Series, Vol. II, p. 281.
Easter Song:
RILEY AND GAYNOR, *Songs of the Child World*, p. 44.
On Easter Day — Old Melody:
SURETTE, *Rote Songs*, p. 51.

MAY DAY

In May:
SURETTE, *Rote Songs*, p. 5.
In May Time:
Progressive Music Series, Teacher's Manual, Vol. I, p. 291.
May Day:
Progressive Music Series, Teacher's Manual, Vol. II, p. 177.
May-pole Dance:
Progressive Music Series, Teacher's Manual, Vol. I, p. 227.

NEW YEAR

Dame Get Up and Bake Your Pies:
NEWMAN, *The Children's Own Book*, p. 34.
Happy New Year:
SURETTE, *Rote Songs*, p. 49.
Happy New Year — (French Folk-song):
Progressive Series, Teacher's Manual, Vol. I, p. 270.

ST. VALENTINE'S DAY

Valentine for Grandma:
Progressive Music Series, Teacher's Manual, p. 155.
Recipe for a Valentine — (Old English Song):
Progressive Music Series, Teacher's Manual, Vol. I, p. 232.
St. Valentine's Day:
SURETTE, *Rote Songs*, p. 50.
Valentine Song:
Progressive Music Series, Teacher's Manual, Vol. I, p. 216.

Thanksgiving **Day:**
Progressive Music Series, Teacher's Manual, Vol. I, p. 284.
Thanksgiving Day — (French):
SURETTE, *Rote Songs,* p. 82.
Thanksgiving Song:
RILEY AND GAYNOR, *Songs of the Child-World,* p. 67.

(c) Directions for Phrasing, Motive, Design and Form

The songs to be used as illustrations for this purpose are listed in Chapter XI, " First Songs for the Children to Play."

The most direct way of introducing this subject is by illustrating the rhythmical connection between music and poetry and by expressing them together, which enables the child-mind to realize that the Rhythmic Law results in the same order and design, symmetry and variety for both. Again, the folk-songs serve best for the reasons previously given; and as those listed in Chapter XI, " First Songs for the Children to Sing," are graded, they are used for the illustration of the above as well as for Rhythmic Form and Design.

The teacher now tells the children that they are to swing, punctuate, and give the same meaning to music as to poetry, and asks them to read several of the folk-song poems, as, for example, the words of the song " Cuckoo " (p. 102), " Come and Dance on the Hillside " and " Bye, Baby, Bye " (see following page); that they are to swing when they feel the rhythm and observe the punctuation marks by slight pauses. In doing this they will discover that there are accented words which change the swing, and that a pause is necessary at the end of each phrase, the length of such pause depending upon the meaning or upon the kind of punctuation mark used — a longer one for a period, a shorter one for a comma.

The teacher then plays the song for the children to swing and sing, asking them to listen for the end of each phrase and tell whether it is complete or incomplete. If complete, it will end at " home " where a period or longer pause is felt; if incomplete, it will end on any of the other tones of the scale — one of the moving tones where a comma or shorter pause is felt.

Other discoveries are soon made; namely, that the majority of phrases consist of four measures within which are to be found little motifs which are frequently repeated in the same or another harmony (illustrations follow in the song " Cuckoo "), after which there are also pauses of varying lengths.   These motives may be compared to the designs in tapestry or embroidery.

COME AND DANCE ON THE HILLSIDE

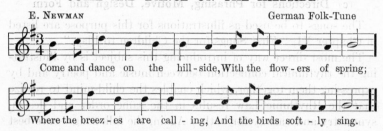

BYE, BABY, BYE

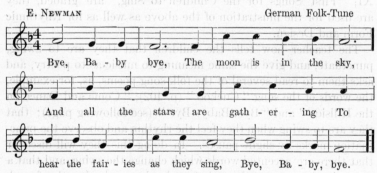

Musical Illustration

In analyzing the folk-song " Cuckoo," the children will observe that the little motive " Cuckoo " is repeated and that these two calls comprise one-half of the phrase through which there is the feeling of another swing beyond the one for each motif, as

Variety is secured in the other half of the phrase by a contrasting motif — " Calls from the Wood," in which one swing is again felt beyond the two swings (one for each of the measures).

Calls from the wood.

A larger feeling of " Oneness " holds these parts together which can be illustrated only as the feeling of a swing through the entire phrase and in which the whole meaning is to be felt and realized from the beginning.

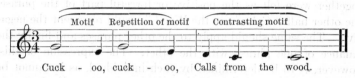

Cuck - oo, cuck - oo, Calls from the wood.

In this phrase there is symmetry of design, a " regular rhythmic pattern " (see next page), in which the swing begins on the first beat of each measure and ends on the third, establishing order and balance. This same symmetry of design with its corresponding variety continues through the three parts, thereby giving form to the composition as a whole.

In Part II, there is a contrasting phrase composed of a motif and its repetition:

and Part III is a repetition of Part I,

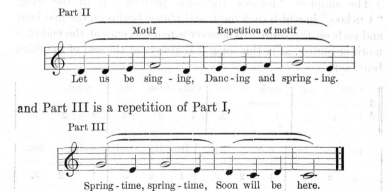

Part II

Let us be sing - ing, Danc - ing and spring - ing.

Part III

Spring - time, spring - time, Soon will be here.

In order to realize the rhythm or " Oneness " of the whole, an illustration is given to the children of the feeling of another swing in which the rhythm of every part continues through the entire composition.

For an artistic expression of this song, the parts are to be balanced and varied as the meaning would suggest. It is helpful to compare this to the Universal law of balance where there is both action and reaction, motion and rest, positive and negative force.

Illustration by Means of the Foregoing Song

The two motifs " Cuckoo," should balance each other and be expressed differently, one as the echo of the other; or, if these two together were felt as the positive or forceful part of the phrase, the other half " Calls from the Wood," would represent the negative.   The same should apply to the other phrases and finally the balance of one phrase with the other.   The expression of this, however, is to be determined by each individual, as it cannot be taught; it can be the result only of the expression of a feeling or mood similar to that of the inspiration of the composer at the time the song was written.

(d) Rhythmic Patterns

The Rhythmic Pattern is determined by the beat upon which the motifs or phrases begin and end, or upon the word or syllable on which the strong beat or accent falls.   It may be either regular or irregular.

The simplest " regular rhythmic pattern " is in the song, " Cuckoo," in which each motif and phrase begins on the first beat and ends on the third.   Whenever a pause occurs at the end of a motif or phrase, as in this song, it is always at the end of the third beat, as:

Cuck - oo,	cuck - oo,	Calls from the	wood.
3/4 1 2 3,	1 2 3,	1 2 3	1 2 3.

Let us be	sing - ing,	Danc-ing and	spring - ing,
1 2 3	1 2 3,	1 2 3	1 2 3,

Spring - time,	spring - time,	Soon will be	here.
1　2　3	1　2　3,	1　2　3	1　2　3

In the folk-song " Come and Dance on the Hillside," the rhythmic pattern is regular, the design being 3 | 1 2, 3 | 1 2, beginning on the third beat and ending on the second in each motive and phrase, as:

¾	Come and	dance on the	hill - side, With the
	3	1　2　3	1　2,　3

flow - ers of	spring, Where the	breez - es are
1　2　3	1　2;　3	1　2　3

call - ing, And the	birds soft - ly	sing.
1　2,　3	1　2　3	1　2.

The following is an illustration of an irregular " rhythmic pattern " within which two different patterns are to be found, one beginning on the first beat, the other on the fourth.

4/4	Bye, ba - by,	bye! The	moon is in the	sky;
	1　2　3　4	1 2 3　4	1　2　3　4	1 2 3;

And	all the stars are	gath - er - ing, To	hear the fair - ies
4	1　2　3　4	1　2　3,　4	1　2　3　4

as they sing,	Bye, ba - by,	bye!
1　2　3　4,	1　2　3　4	1　2　3　4

In this song there is also an exception to the usual four-measure phrase as the song ends with a phrase of two measures.

As other songs are analyzed, the discovery will be made that the same rhythmic principle applies to all songs no matter what their time-signature may be.

CHAPTER IV

RHYTHM (Concluded)

Duration of Tones — Rhythmic Notation — Original Expression of Rhythmic Phrases

This subject is introduced very early in the class lessons and simultaneously with Pitch and the Rhythmic games, as it leads to a feeling of Tone-duration, and enables the children to create melodies rhythmically and express them by means of their proper note values.

(a) Duration of Tones — The Stepping of Note Values

Directions. — The children step to the tones as they sing, by holding the step as long as each tone is held with the voice.

LIST OF SONGS FOR STEPPING TO SINGING

This is Little Yellow Head:
  NEIDLINGER, *Small Songs for Small Singers*, p. 53.
Mr. Squirrel:
  NEIDLINGER, *Small Songs for Small Singers*, p. 38.
Tiddlely Winks and Tiddlely Wee:
  NEIDLINGER, *Small Songs for Small Singers*, p. 19.
The Caterpillar:
  NEIDLINGER, *Small Songs for Small Singers*, p. 18.
Goosey Goosey Gander:
  MOFFAT, *Little Songs of Long Ago*, p. 59.
Dancing Raindrops:
  Progressive Music Series, Teacher's Manual, Vol. I, p. 228.
Who Am I?
  Progressive Music Series, Teacher's Manual, Vol. I, p. 286.
Woodland Lessons — (Swedish Folk-dance):
  Progressive Music Series, Vol. II, p. 187.

A Game for Recognizing Songs by Tapping the Rhythm*

The children form a circle about one child who holds a cane which is to be used for tapping the rhythm of any song that has been used in class work.   While the child in the center is choosing a song, the children in the circle sing:

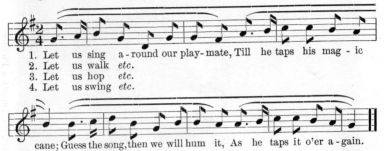

1. Let   us sing   a - round our play-mate, Till   he taps   his   mag - ic
2. Let   us walk   *etc.*
3. Let   us hop   *etc.*
4. Let   us swing *etc.*

cane; Guess the song, then we will hum   it, As   he taps it o'er a - gain.

The child in the center then taps the rhythm of the song chosen as the others listen attentively to be able to name it.   After it is known, all sing to the tapping.   The child who first guessed correctly is in the center when the game is repeated.

(b) Rhythmic Notation

STEPPING TO SINGING

This subject includes the Stepping to Singing, the Drawing of Duration Pictures and Rhythmic Phrases, and the Writing of Note Values.

DIRECTIONS

1. The children step while singing, holding each step as long as the tone is held by the voice, turning at the end of each phrase and stepping in the opposite direction.

NOTE. — It has been found more simple to use the quarter note as the unit of measurement.   The word "long" is used for the half note or the tone representing two claps.   The words "very long" are used for the whole note or the tone that is held for four claps, and also for the dotted half notes. The words "very short" are used for the eighth notes in which two tones are sung for each clap.

---

* This singing game was suggested by the "Guessing Game" in G. Walker and H. S. Jenks' "Songs and Games," published by Oliver Ditson Co.

Stepping the Note Values and Drawing the Duration Picture

The teacher also gives any original illustrations to assist the children in realizing fully the difference in the values of these notes. The one most frequently used is the drawing of an orange or an apple and dividing the whole into halves, quarters and eighths, and comparing the sizes of the parts to the length of the tones held.

2. The children step while singing the length of the tones as in the song:

Swing-ing low, Swing-ing high, Through the air we gai - ly fly.

they step while singing,

Short short long, short short long.

then in the opposite direction for the next phrase.

Short short short short short short long.

DURATION PICTURES

3. While the class sings, one child writes rhythmically a " Duration Picture " on the board, in which each line is prolonged as long as its corresponding tone is held by the voice. Thus the length of the steps is sung to the melody of the song, as:

Short	short	long,	short	short	long,

Short	short	short	short	short	short	long.

4. For adding the bar lines:

The teacher tells the class that a bar line is placed before the strong pulse or word that begins each swing, or at the place where the swing changes. The children feel this by swinging and singing.

5. While the class swings and sings, one child (also swinging with the left hand) places a dot under each line representing the strong pulse, at the word beginning each swing.

6. In the same way, bar lines are placed before each dotted line and double bar lines at the beginning and at the end, after which the dots are erased.

7. While the class sings, another child adds stems rhythmically to the Duration lines:

8. The children clap the time according to the directions given in Chapter III, under " Directions for Discovering the Time," in order to find out the time of the Time signature which is then added.

WRITING OF NOTE VALUES

9. The class is now told that the word " short " or the tone that is given one clap is a ♩ quarter note, and that the word " long " or the tone that is given two claps is a ♩ half note. The children step again and sing the names of the note values to the melody:

Quarter, quarter, half, quarter, quarter, half.

Quarter, quarter, quarter, quarter, quarter, quarter, half.

10. While the class sings, one child adds the note values to the duration picture.

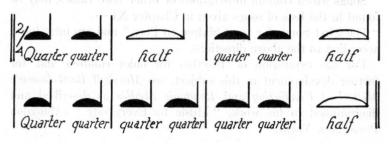

LIST OF SONGS

The songs for this purpose will be found carefully graded in " The Children's Own Book."

The following are especially suggested:

Songs containing ♩ and ♩ notes:
Come and Sing a Song to Me.
Sunshine Bright.
Swinging.
Bye-lo, Dolly Dear.

Songs containing 𝅗𝅥 — ♩ and ♩ notes:
Wee Son, John.
Springtime.
Hum, hum, hum.

Songs containing ♩ — ♩ and ♩. notes:
Little Blue Pigeon.
Pat-a-cake.
Cuckoo.
Bye-Baby-Bye.

Songs containing ♩ — ♩ and ♪ notes:
Hot Cross Buns.
The Nightingale.
Make Hay by the Neckar.

Songs containing ♩ — ♩ — ♪ and ♩. notes:
Hymn of Praise.
A Rooster and a Gander.
Pretty Little Hildegarde.

Songs for Illustrating the Remaining Note Values

Songs which contain illustrations of other note values, may be found in the lists of songs given in Chapter XI — "The First Songs for the Children to Play," and are introduced according to the above directions.

For the expression of Rhythm for older children and for further development in this subject, see *Marshall Bartholomew's Method of Conducting* and *Rhythmic Studies* as described and diagrammed in his work, "Music for Everybody" (Abingdon Press, New York).

(c) Original Expression of Rhythmic Phrases

Directions:

1. The teacher writes the Time-signature and the note values to be used on the board, thus:

and taps rhythmically with chalk or cane while pointing to the above formula, a four or an eight-measure phrase. The first beat of each measure must be accented.

2. The children close their eyes and each improvises a melody with or without words for the phrase. If they are unable to do this, the teacher improvises a melody at the piano in the given rhythm to which the children swing and create their own words.

3. Each child swings and sings his song, steps the note values, and then writes these note values of the rhythmic phrase in his tablet, thus:

If the work in Notation, Pitch and Key-signature has been given simultaneously with this subject, the children will be able to write these phrases in any key in their blank music-books.

The teacher repeats the above process by gradually adding other note values, Rests and Time-signatures until the children can create and write freely in all.

ILLUSTRATIONS

Different Methods to be Used in Following the Foregoing Directions

1. One of the children creates a Rhythmic phrase and, following the formula at the board, taps it with a cane or with chalk for the others of the class to swing, step and write.

2. The teacher creates Rhythmic phrases and writes the note values on the board as:

The children improvise melodies for these phrases with or without words which they sing, swing and write.

3. Each child creates and writes the note values for a Rhythmic phrase on the board for the rest of the class to sing, swing and write.

4. The teacher improvises at the keyboard a Rhythmic phrase containing the familiar note values, and the children, after listening attentively, write the note values of the phrase in their tablets.

5. Each child, if possible, improvises a Rhythmic phrase at the piano for the others of the class to write.

6. The teacher plays folk-dances from *Burchenal and Crampton*, Folk-dance Album, Progressive Music Series, (Silver, Burdette Co.), Folk-dances of Denmark and Sweden, *Surette* Rote Songs, and any of the other folk-song or folk-dance albums listed in " Lists of Books for Teachers " (this volume) omitting the words if a folk-song is chosen. The children swing the rhythm while humming the melody, create words for the music, step the note values, and write the duration pictures and the note values in rhythmic phrases in their blank music-books.

7. Each child creates a dance composed of one or more rhythmic phrases, swings and hums it for the teacher to play and for the rest of the class to sing, swing, dance and write.

If the class is ready for melodic and harmonic dictation, the teacher dictates these dances according to the directions given under the special subjects of Melody and Harmony, after which the children finger the songs while singing them away from the keyboard, and play them in any of the twelve keys.

CHAPTER V

HOME-TONE OR KEYNOTE

At the very beginning of the class lessons, the children are made to feel that there are motion and rest tones. This is done by means of illustrations. For example, it is explained that songs may be compared to children who play away from their homes, but to which they always return for rest.

To develop this feeling or " home " consciousness, the teacher plays any of the songs familiar to the class, stops before the " home-tone " has been reached and asks if they feel satisfied, or if the songs seem finished; if not, to finish them by singing the tone that would bring each melody " home."

Further illustrations show how " homes " may be changed by playing the same songs in different keys. This gives the first feeling of transposition.*

The following " Home-tone Drills and Games," have been successfully used.

DRILL I

The teacher plays the scale and asks the children to listen and tell her the rest and motion tones it contains. The rest-tone below and above may be described as the downstairs and the upstairs of the same home. She does the same in many keys.

DRILL II
INCLUDING THE "ECHO GAME"

The teacher plays a phrase of a folk-song that ends at home, stops before the last tone and asks the class to sing it. To make a *game* of this, the children may take turns echoing from a corner the tone the class sings. Many such phrases should be used and played in different keys.

The following is a list of songs in which the first phrase of each ends on the home tone.

* Here, as always, whenever possible, topics should be related to life.

These songs will all be found in " The Children's Own Book."
Au Claire de la Lune.
Hum, hum, hum.
Cuckoo.
Hop, hop, hop.
Ah! vous dirai-je maman.
The Nightingale.
Oh Mountain Pine.
Where are You Going?

DRILL III

The teacher creates melodies, plays them and asks the children to find and sing the " home-tones." The Echo Game, described in the previous drill, is repeated for the benefit of the children who are still unable to recognize the " home-tone " readily.

DRILL IV

The children create songs that come " home."

DRILL V

The teacher writes a verse on the board; as " My bed is like a little boat " (*Stevenson*). The children close their eyes, become very still, then create melodies for the words, that come home.

DRILL VI

Questions and Answers which may also be used as illustrations for Phrasing.

The teacher sings a musical question and a child answers in the same rhythm. Singing the answer will bring the children to a feeling of rest on the " home-tone " as does a period at the end of a sentence. Words are also used for original melodies for the drill of questions and answers. These may be created or chosen from any of the well known books of poetry for children, as those listed in " Books for Verses, Chapter VI, Creative Work."

Illustrations from Nursery rhymes are:

Bah, bah, black sheep, have you any wool?
Yes sir, yes sir, three bags full.

Pat-a-cake, pat-a-cake, baker's man;
So I will, master, as fast as I can.

Where are you going, my pretty maid?
I'm going a-milking, sir, she said.

Bow-wow-wow, whose dog art thou?
Little Tom Tucker's dog, bow-bow-wow.

Goosey, goosey, gander, where shall I wander?
Upstairs and downstairs and in my lady's chamber.

Sing, sing, what shall I sing?
The cat's run away with the pudding-bag string.

GAME I

To make a game of the above, let each child, in turn, sing a question, pointing to another child for an answer. This one then makes up a question and points to another for the answer; and so on until all in the class have been called upon.

A LETTER–BOX GAME

(CREATED BY MILDRED RIDER)

The teacher draws the picture of a letter-box on the board after which she plays folk-songs and " Make-up " songs. Whenever the home-tone is reached, at the end of a phrase in the song, each child, in turn, mails a letter by drawing a tiny picture of one inside the box.

CHAPTER VI

CREATIVE WORK

"The function of the teacher is to bring into the daily life of the child the music that is in his heart, because it is also in the heart of nature." — EDMOND HOLMES.
"A poet sees down into the heart of things — a true musician hears down into the heart of things." — F. D. DAVIES.

The old methods aimed mostly at making performers; the new method must make composers. The old method laid stress upon the cumulation of knowledge from without; the new method places first stress upon the liberation of musical feeling from within. The old method was based on the efficiency of the teacher; the new, on the efficiency of the child. In the new method we are seeking for the emancipation of childhood from the machine-like shackles of the old; we are seeking to let the child feel early that his musical education is rather the liberation of the music within him by delightful work and play, than an accumulation from without of knowledge *about* music; that musical feeling and knowledge grow from within each individual as life from a seed; as water bubbles from a fountain, and that any system of teaching music which checks the free creative action of life is a mistaken system.

The teacher of the new method must be keen to the fact that the child must first be encouraged to feel music; to let his feelings expand from within, taking forms by a process of growth which is true to his own individuality; and that, while the knowledge about music and its necessary technique for performance must follow in due time, that all this later equipment must be based upon the earlier feeling and individuality. In short, that the child's emotional nature and sense of music should precede, dominate and preside over his later skill and technique on instruments. Just as in civilization the industrial machine ought to be for man, and not man for the machine, so in music, the instrument should be for the child, and not the child for the instrument.

DIRECTIONS

In order to develop this freedom of expression and originality from the very beginning of class work, the teacher asks the children to create their own songs — both words and melodies. They enjoy this, particularly when they can hear them played by the teacher and sung by the class. They are then asked to sing about anything that makes them happy. Illustrations by means of suggestions and questions follow on the powers, qualities and limitations of certain musical instruments, showing that music cannot come from any one of them until it first exists in the heart and mind of the one who gave it musical expression and that it is then only expressed at the keyboard as it was felt and heard. The child can be shown that the simplest musical feeling truly expressed, represents both art and beauty.

If the " home-tone " and " rhythmic feeling " have been well established in the children's consciousness, illustrations of verses are given (and used simultaneously with their own), in order that the same swing will be felt in poetry as in music. This also gives them a standard for creating their own verse according to the laws of rhythm and rhyme.

To Illustrate this Connection Between Poetry and Music

In the poetic phrases given, the teacher has the children determine, by swinging, the most important word or syllable on which the accent or strong pulse falls and feel how the swing changing at this place is the same for both the verse and the melody, and that it follows the same " rhythmic pattern."

In leading to the expression of these verses at the keyboard, the teacher follows the same directions as those given under the separate subjects of Rhythm, Melody and Harmony, namely:

Rhythm, Chapters III and IV.
Melody, Chapter VIII.
Harmony, Chapter X.
First Songs for the Children to Play, Chapter XI.

BOOKS FOR VERSES

CADY, CALVIN B.   Music Education, Book II, *C. F. Summy Co., Chicago.*
CARROLL, LEWIS.   Alice's Adventures in Wonderland.
FIELD, EUGENE.   A Child's Garland of Verses — Bedtime Rhymes.
KIPLING, RUDYARD.   Just-so-Stories, *Doubleday Page & Co., New York.*
MOTHER GOOSE RHYMES
PALGRAVE, FRANCIS TURNER (Editor).   Children's Treasury of Lyrical Poetry, *Macmillan, London.*
PALGRAVE, FRANCIS TURNER (Editor).   Palgrave's Golden Treasury, *Dent, London.*
STEVENSON, R. L.   Child's Garden of Verse.
TENNYSON, ALFRED.   Poems.   (Those relating to Childhood.)
LANIER, SIDNEY.   Science of English Verse.   (A book for teachers on rhythmic study) *Chas. Scribner, New York.*

Illustrations of Verses to be Given the Children for Original Melodies

Spring is here.
March, boys, march!
Ding, dong, bell.
Dolly, close your eyes.
Robin, sing to me!
Sing and dance with me.
Row, boatman, row!
Sleep, my pretty one, sleep!
Gently rock my dolly dear.

Slowly sail the clouds on high.
Far away the robin sings.
The stars are lamps that shine at night.
The stars are twinkling in the skies. — *Field*.
The shepherd loves his tiny sheep. — *Field*.
The earth is lost in slumbers deep. — *Field*.
Boys and girls, come out to play. — *Nursery Rhymes*.
All night! Across the dark we steer. — *Stevenson*.
The sea is singing to the sands. — *Field*.
Nightly sings the staring owl. — *Shakespeare*.
The old moon laughed and sang a song. — *Stevenson*.
My bed is like a little boat. — *Stevenson*.
For me the bees came by to sing. — *Stevenson*.
Sleep, little pigeon, and fold your wings. — *Field*.
In through the window a moonbeam comes. — *Field*.
The moon has a face like the clock in the hall. — *Stevenson*.
I'd like to go to Afriky an' hunt the lions there. — *Field*.
The camel's hump is an ugly lump. — *Kipling*.
I saw a ship a-sailing, a-sailing on the sea. — *Sugar and Spice*.
Winnie and Minnie slept in a shell. — *Tennyson*.
I woke before the morning, I was happy all the day. — *Stevenson*.
Tom would be a driver and Maria go to sea. — *Stevenson*.
Waves are on the meadow like the waves there are at sea. — *Stevenson*.
The Dinkey-Bird goes singing, in the amfalula tree. — *Field*.
I have a little shadow that goes in and out with me. — *Stevenson*.

Every evening, after tea,
Teeny-Weeny comes to me. — *Field*.

I am singing to the sheep,
As they rock the lambs to sleep. — *Field*.

Over hill and over plain.
Soon will speed the shut-eye train. — *Field*.

Shut-eye train is passing fair —
Golden dreams await us there. — *Field*.

Beside his loving mother-sheep
A little lambkin is asleep. — *Field.*

There are two stars in yonder steeps
That watch the baby while he sleeps. — *Field.*

I saw the high, the silver sky,
Down in a pavement pool! — *Mary White Slater.*

I should like to rise and go
Where the golden apples grow. — *Stevenson.*

Happy hearts and happy faces,
Happy play in grassy places. — *Stevenson.*

I have just to shut my eyes,
To go sailing through the skies. — *Stevenson.*

When children are happy and lonely and good,
The friend of the children comes out of the wood. — *Stevenson.*

I have to go to bed and see
The birds still hopping on the tree. — *Stevenson.*

O wind, a-blowing all day long,
O wind, that sings so loud a song! — *Stevenson.*

My little dog whose name is Tan
Can run as fast as any man.

The organ with the organ man
Is singing in the rain. — *Stevenson.*

Toot! toot! the whistle blows!
Away to work my father goes.

The world is so full of a number of things
I'm sure we should all be as happy as kings. — *Stevenson.*

Hush-a-bye, baby,
On the tree-top,
When the wind blows
The cradle will rock. — *Nursery Rhymes.*

Little boy blue,
Come blow your horn,
The sheep's in the meadow,
The cow's in the corn. — *Nursery Rhymes.*

Dickery, dickery, dock,
The mouse ran up the clock,
The clock struck one, the mouse ran down,
Dickery, dickery, dock. — *Nursery Rhymes.*

The day — the day — the shining day
When happy winds were blowing,
And down the shady garden way
The cherry flowers were snowing. — *Mary White Slater.*

Of speckled eggs the birdie sings
And nests among the trees;
The sailor sings of ropes and things
In ships upon the seas. — *Stevenson.*

A birdie with a yellow bill
Hopped upon the window sill,
Cocked his shining eye and said,
" Aint you 'shamed, you sleepy-head?" — *Stevenson.*

Dark brown is the river,
Golden is the sand,
It flows along forever
With trees on either hand. — *Stevenson.*

Bring the comb and play upon it,
Marching here we come;
Willie cocks his Highland bonnet,
Johnnie beats the drum. — *Stevenson.*

How do you like to go up in a swing,
Up in the air so blue?
Oh, I do think it the pleasantest thing.
Ever a child can do. — *Stevenson.*

Musical Letters and Postman Game

MUSICAL LETTERS

The teacher asks each child to create a musical letter, namely, a verse and melody, written in the form of a " pitch " and " duration picture," and to address it to one of the children in the class, as:

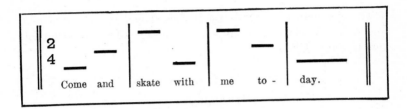

The letters are written in class until the children are able to write them without the teacher's assistance, after which they are assigned for " home-work."

When in envelopes and addressed, they are dropped in the postman's bag, for use and distribution in the following game.

POSTMAN GAME*

One child, pretending to be the postman, comes from the far side of the room carrying the music-bag (postman's bag), containing the letters. As he approaches the class he sings:

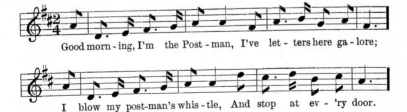

* This singing game was suggested by the "Postman Song" in Fanny Knowlton's "Nature Songs for Children," published by Milton Bradley Company.

The class answers:

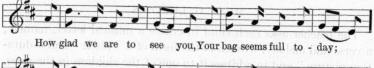

How glad we are to see you, Your bag seems full to - day;

Please give us each a let - ter, Be - fore you go a - way.

The Postman distributes the letters which the children read and sing. At the Christmas season the same idea is used for letters to Santa Claus.

CHAPTER VII

THE SCALE

Since the scale is the basis of all melodic thought, it is necessary to awaken an interest in it that there may develop a clear consciousness of this usually most disliked subject. So a song is made of it which delights the children, particularly when they find they can sing their own words to the melody and make the whole expression rhythmical and musical.

There is one "Major" scale and three "Minors" — the so-called Natural or Normal, Harmonic, and Melodic Minors, which three are alterations of the Major.

ILLUSTRATIONS

C Major scale

The A Minor scales related to C Major

Natural or Normal Minor   Harmonic Minor

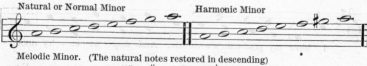

Melodic Minor. (The natural notes restored in descending)

This one long song, as the Major scale is called, as well as the one long song for each Minor (the Natural, Harmonic and Melodic) can be sung on any one of the seven white or five black keys without an error provided the songs are really heard and the feeling of the distance between tones established.

A Plan for Introducing the Scale

THE MAJOR SCALE

1. The teacher tells the children that she intends to play the tones of a song to which they may later fill in words and swing and sing. She then plays the C Major scale very slowly; and, in order to get as much free expression as possible from the children asks if any difference in tone is felt. This is to lead them to discover for themselves that some tones give a feeling of rest and others of motion.

2. To establish this feeling more definitely, the teacher speaks of the song as one that is made up of *rest* and *motion* tones, explaining that each tone differs from the others as do the separate colors of the rainbow, and bids the class listen again that they may be able to describe the feeling each tone gives.

She plays middle C and asks what that tone means to them. Of the two feelings of rest and motion, they will usually respond with that of rest; if not, she plays the scale down, stops at D and has them sing middle C.

She then plays D. Here the children feel the desire to move, recognize the tone as a different quality from C and higher. She repeats this process with all of the other tones until the octave C is reached, when the children again recognize the same quality of tone and feeling of rest that the first C gave, the only distinction being that one is higher than the other. This may be made an illustration and related to life by explaining that home is the same whether downstairs or upstairs. And further that the " downstairs " or first tone of the scale is to be distinguished by 1 and the upstairs by 1̄. One child is then asked to write these numbers on the board at some distance apart while they are played by the teacher and sung by the class. The result will be as follows:

1

As the teacher plays the other (motion) tones of the scale and the class sings them, another child is chosen to fill in the numbers in order that they may discover by writing that there are seven different tones in the scale:

1̄
7
6
5
4
3
2
1̲

3. A song is then made of these tones by using poetry that will make both melody and words swing to the same rhythm. The teacher asks the children to create their own verse, but also gives them illustrations of suitable forms from the best Children's Poetry in order that they may have a standard from which to work.

The best rhythm to keep the song simple and the tones of even value, is that in which the swing begins on the second word or syllable as:

I saw you toss the kites on high, And blow the birds a - bout the sky.

The following are verses of the same rhythm by Robert Louis Stevenson:

A child should always say what's true,
And speak when he is spoken to.

Whenever Auntie moves around
Her dresses make a curious sound.

Close by the jolly fire I sit
To warm my frozen bones a bit.

My bed is like a little boat,
Nurse helps me in when I embark.

In winter I get up at night
And dress by yellow candle light.
In summer quite the other way
I have to go to bed by day.

Original Verses by Children

My pussy's fur is soft as silk,
When I have dinner, she has milk.

As I climbed up the apple-tree
A big red apple fell on me.

Let's plant some seeds all in a row
And see if we can watch them grow.

On Christmas day I find the toys
That Santa brings to girls and boys.

Directions for Making a Pitch* and Duration Picture,† and a Rhythmic Pattern‡ of the Above

While singing the song rhythmically, the children swing, make the Pitch Picture with their hands, draw the Pitch Picture on the board, step the note values, draw the Duration Picture, swing and add the bar lines, add the stems to the Duration lines, clap the time, and write the note values.

* See Chapter VIII, p. 63.
† See Chapter IV, Rhythmic Notation, p. 29.
‡ See Chapter III, p. 14.

The following will be the result:

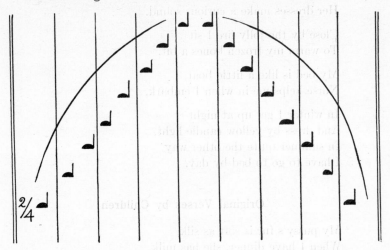

GAME

A MUSICAL SPELLING–MATCH

5. A game for testing the ability of each child to carry the melody of the scale-song.

Directions. — The correct tones in the scale are sung as words are spelt in a " spelling-match." Each child is given a turn in singing one of the successive tones of the scale, and later, four tones. The teacher gives a new key-note or " home-tone " whenever the song is repeated, and the words for any of the scale-songs or " la " are used with the melody. When a child fails to sing correctly, he is considered out of the game until it is repeated. The child wins who has made no error, after all of the others have been forced out of the game by the singing of incorrect tones.

THE EXPRESSION OF THE SCALE–SONG AT THE KEYBOARD

6. Each child, in turn, is asked to express this song at the keyboard, by beginning on any of the five black or seven white keys; to sing each tone before it is played and to listen for its quality and distance so that when heard, it will correspond with or "match" the voice.

The children will make the " discovery " that some of the tones are farther apart than others and that the difference between them is: A " step-over,"* or " whole tone " for some, which, in this volume, for convenience, will be called a *Step* and the " half-tone " for others which will be called a *Slide* (half-step).

7. For hearing the exact distance between the " steps " and " slides," the teacher is advised to improvise Games and Drills.

ILLUSTRATION OF A GAME
(CREATED BY MILDRED RIDER)

One child pretending to be a great musician is seated at the piano. Another playing " mother " brings her child to have his ability for hearing " steps " and " slides " tested. The musician strikes any tone within the Middle C octave and asks the pupil to sing a " step " and then a " slide " from that tone. This child then becomes the musician and the game is repeated until all the children have had an opportunity to sing a number of whole and half-steps.

ILLUSTRATION OF A DRILL

The teacher tells the children that going up the scale may be compared to the climbing of a ladder except that the rungs are not always placed at an even distance apart. As the scale is played very slowly, the children sing and listen discovering for themselves when the lines are to be placed at a greater distance apart for the " steps " and at a shorter distance for the " slides." Each child, in turn, draws one of the lines or " rungs " while all sing and listen.

The result will be the following:

* In a "step-over" the next note on the keyboard is omitted.

The above directions are followed in the drawing of a new " Pitch " and " Duration " picture in which the lines are drawn at a greater distance for the " steps " and at a lesser distance for the " slides," as:

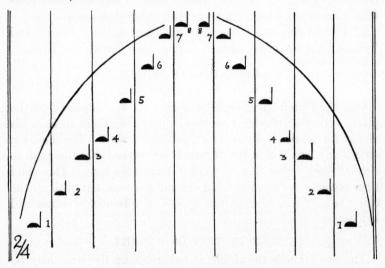

SUBSTITUTION OF NOTES FOR TONES AND NUMBERS

8. The children have previously discovered that there are seven tones in the one long scale-song and that, therefore, only seven letters of the alphabet are necessary to express them, namely, a-b-c-d-e-f-g. When, however, this song is transposed (or the " home " changed) the letters are to follow consecutively, and, in order to keep the " steps " and " slides " in their fixed places in the song, *sharps* or *flats* are needed. The teacher explains that the sharp, ♯, is always to be found a " slide " above the tone considered and the flat, ♭, a " slide " below.

The children now write their own scales by writing the letters of which they are composed above the " Pitch " and " Duration Pictures," or at the side of the illustration of the ladder. They begin with any letter or " home-tone " and while singing and listening discover for themselves when a ♯ or ♭ is necessary to form

the required " step " or " slide." From the number of different
sharps or flats used in the formation of each scale, they discover
the Key-Signature, thus:

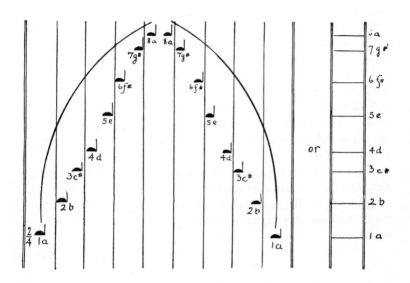

In the above scale on A (home), the Key-Signature is found to be
f♯, c♯ and g♯.

As a preparation for expressing the above rhythmically at the
keyboard, the children devise their own fingering by pretending
to play in the air while singing the song first to the letters and then
to any of the verses they prefer to use. The teacher gives the
necessary guidance in order that the thumb will not be placed on
a black key and so the fingering will permit of as much smoothness
as possible.

The same is then expressed rhythmically at the keyboard by
each child in turn, as all sing and swing to the letters and the
words.

9. This plan is followed for the formation of the other eleven
scales.

Order and System in Scale Formation

10. To understand the order and system involved in the scale formation, the teacher asks the children to construct, finger, write and play the scales in their regular order in the circle of keys. (See the following illustration, p. 57.)

Beginning at C at the uppermost part of the circle, divisions are made for the six scales containing sharp signatures, to be placed on one-half of the circle and the six scales containing flats on the other half. The progression continues regularly, the next scale always beginning on the fifth tone of the preceding one. At the end of the first half of the circle an " enharmonic " change is made — that is, f♯ is called g♭ and the progression continues in the same order in the flat signature scales until the circle is completed at C.

The children will discover that in the progression of the sharp signatures one sharp is always added which is found on the seventh tone of each scale, and that a flat is always dropped in the progression of the flat signatures which comes on the fourth tone of each scale.

enharmonic
change

8	c	g	d	a	e	b	f♯ g♭	d♭	a♭	e♭	b♭	f♭	c
7	b	f♯	c♯	g♯	d♯	a♯	e♯ f	c	g	d	a	e	b
6	a	e	b	f♯	c♯	g♯	d♯ e♭	b♭	f	c	g	d	a
5	g	d	a	e	b	f♯	c♯ d♭	a♭	e♭	b♭	f	c	g
4	f	c	g	d	a	e	b c♭	g♭	d♭	a♭	e♭	b♭	f
3	e	b	f♯	c♯	g♯	d♯	a♯ b♭	f	c	g	d	a	e
2	d	a	e	b	f♯	c♯	g♯ a♭	e♭	b♭	f	c	g	d
1	c	g	d	a	e	b	f♯ g♭	d♭	a♭	e♭	b♭	f	c

enharmonic
change

CIRCLE OF KEYS AND KEY SIGNATURES

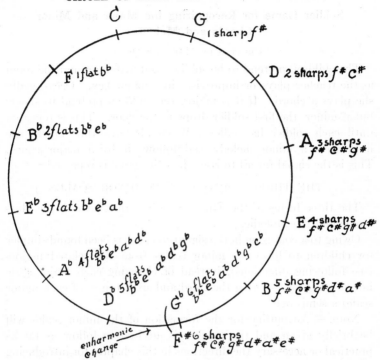

For further directions of this topic, see Scale Notation, Major, Chapter IX, The Scale.

THE MINOR SCALE

1. The teacher plays a major and then a minor chord on any of the twelve different keys and the children sing the roots and describe the feeling each chord gives. Answers such as bright and dull, light and dark, day and night, sun and moon, have been given by the children.

2. The teacher plays a major and a harmonic minor scale and asks the children to listen and tell the order in which they were played and the feeling each gives.

3. She plays folk-songs and folk-dances and any of the classics in major and minor modes and asks the children to name the mode of each.

GAME

Soldier Game for Recognizing the Major and Minor Chords and Melodies

(CREATED BY MARJORIE DICE)

The children pretend to be soldiers and march around the room as the teacher plays or improvises in a major key. Occasionally she plays a chord. If it is major, the children pretend to shoot; but if minor, the first soldier drops to the floor. This is repeated until each soldier has fallen. When all have thus fallen, she improvises a minor melody and follows it by a major chord. This is the signal for all to rise when the game is repeated.

THE THREE FORMS OF THE MINOR SCALE

The three forms of the Minor Scale are the Natural, the Harmonic and the Melodic.

Owing to a confusion in the signatures, it has been found simpler for children to form the minor scales from the related majors (see following directions), instead of changing each major scale into a minor by lowering the third and sixth tones (of each major scale) a semi-tone.

Note. — An outline for the formation of the minor scales will be briefly given and the teacher is advised to follow as far as practical or necessary the directions in this chapter for introducing the major scales.

Directions for Forming the Natural, Harmonic and Melodic Minor Scales

The teacher asks the children to play or write while singing, any of the Major scales — the scale of D for instance.

She tells them that the related minor of every major scale is a " step " and a " slide " (minor third) below the major (" home-tone "), or the sixth tone of the major scale, and that the same Key-Signature is used for both.

They discover that the related minor of D major is B, and that the Key-Signature is the same for both, namely, f♯, c♯.

She then plays the Natural minor scale in B and tells the children that the same tones are used as in the related major scale, asks them to sing it, compose words for it, listen for the slides and steps, sing the letter-names and play it rhythmically, as:

This same scale is then sung and played in all keys.

THE HARMONIC MINOR SCALE

The teacher plays the B Harmonic minor scale very slowly, asks the children to sing each separate tone and to tell her how it differs from the Natural. They will make the discovery that the seventh tone of the Harmonic minor scale has been raised a semitone both in ascending and in descending, and that the result is a "step" and a "slide" between the sixth and the seventh tones. She tells them that this change of tone is designated before the note each time it is written, and not in the Key-Signature; consequently the Key-Signature remains the same as that of the related or major key. They sing the song to the scale-numbers and letter-names.

B Minor Harmonic Scale

As this is the most common form of minor scale used in instrumental music, additional time is given to its development. The children are asked to compose many more verses suitable for this melody and to sing and play it more frequently in all of the keys.

The following words were written by a nine-year-old child:

> When twilight deepens in the sky,
> The dark and silent night is nigh.

MELODIC MINOR SCALE

As the teacher plays the B minor Melodic scale, the children discover that the sixth and seventh tones of the Natural Minor are raised a semitone or "slide" in ascending, while in descending the tones are the same as the "Natural Minor." The signature also remains the same as that of the relative Major, and the change of tone on the sixth and seventh steps is designated by the use of accidentals. These tones are sung and later written to letter-names.

B Minor Melodic Scale

From the above explanations the children are able to construct and play all of the related minor scales and add them to the circle of Major keys they have previously formed.

Thus:

RELATED MINOR KEYS

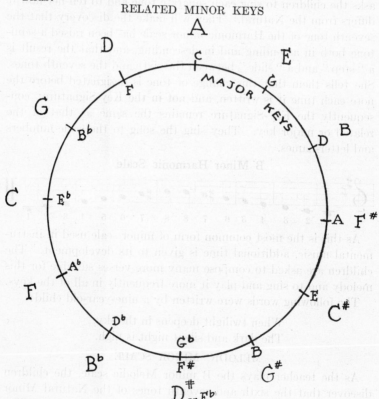

For *Minor Scale Notation*, see " Scale Notation, Minor," Chapter IX, The Scale.

CHAPTER VIII

MELODY

Bulwer Lytton says, " Music once admitted to the soul becomes a sort of spirit and never dies. It wanders perturbedly through the halls and galleries of the memory, and is often heard again distinct and living as when it first displaced the wavelets of the air."

Children can be made so familiar with melody that every experience in life will suggest a song. When the child's musical consciousness is thus developed, a joyous reaction is the result and renewed whenever a melody is recalled. For this reason a large number of rote songs should be learned and sung from the very beginning of musical training and throughout the whole period of study. Consequently, many lists of songs have been given in this volume covering every subject of class work.

The songs of this subject are chosen for two reasons: they not only arouse keen interest in the children, but serve also in leading them gradually to distinguish the high from the low tones — to hear the direction in which the melodies move, namely, up and down, or along the same level; and to hear the exact tones of a song. Eventually they will learn to express them in any key. Many original games are also included for the purpose of obtaining the desired results through play so that the children will not become discouraged by the effort involved.

BEAR AND BIRD GAME

(Created by Mildred Rider)

To Distinguish the High from the Low Tones

The teacher asks the children to tell about the birds and the bears; where they make their homes, etc., after which she improvises bird calls in the treble and bear calls in the bass. As the children hear the bird songs played, they raise their hands, and as they hear the bear calls played, they lower them.

AEROPLANE GAME

(CREATED BY MILDRED RIDER)

For Hearing Tones as They are Repeated and Move Up and Down

The teacher tells the children that a melody moves very much the same as an aeroplane, and asks them to illustrate with their hands the movements of the latter. They do this by moving their hands up and down and along the same level. She then tells them that she will play a melody that is supposed to represent the journey of an aeroplane and that, as she does so they are to follow its direction with their hands. She plays arpeggios, or improvises a melody which has a decided movement up and down and which occasionally repeats the same tones.

GUESSING GAME

For Hearing the Melody as It Moves Up and Down and to Distinguish the High and Low Home-tones in the Same Song

All of the children, except one child who is blindfolded, form a circle; and as they sing, grow tall or short as the song suggests. As the teacher plays the last part of the song they remain quiet and listen, and if the melody ends on the upper home-tone they are tall, on the lower one, small. The blindfolded child telling whether they are tall or small.

The children sing:

The lil - ies grow so tall, The pan - sies grow so small,

Lil - ies tall, Pan - sies small.

The teacher asks, " which are grow-ing now," and plays

or

PITCH PICTURES

By Pitch Pictures is meant the movement of the hands and their written outline as the melodies move.

The children are told that as outlines are drawn for paintings, so they may be drawn for melodies, and followed with the hands moving up and down and along the same level as the songs are sung. For the first Pitch Pictures, songs have been selected which the children enjoy singing and in which parts may be chosen for these pitch outlines.

ILLUSTRATION

The Bee — NEIDLINGER, *Small Songs for Small Singers*, p. 26.

The teacher or the class, or both sing the song, and while buzzing the bee's song which is at the end of the melody, the children make Pitch Pictures with their hands and on the board. The following is the written " Pitch Picture ":

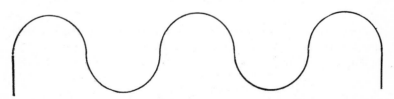

A LIST OF SONGS FOR THE FIRST "PITCH PICTURES"

The Bee — NEIDLINGER, *Small Songs for Small Singers*, p. 26.
    (Pitch picture of the bee's buzz.)
Little Lamb — NEIDLINGER, *Small Songs for Small Singers*, p. 11.
    (Pitch picture of baa.)
The Kitten and the Bow-wow — NEIDLINGER, *Small Songs for Small Singers*,
    p. 1.

(One-half the class sings and makes a pitch picture of the dog's bow-wow; the other half, of the kitten's meow. The teacher sings the rest.)

Tick-tock — NEIDLINGER, *Small Songs for Small Singers*, p. 54.

(Pitch pictures for the tick-tocks.)

The Chicken — NEIDLINGER, *Small Songs for Small Singers*, p. 5.

(Pitch picture of the last phrase which is the scale backwards.)

The Bunny — NEIDLINGER, *Small Songs for Small Singers*, p. 13.

(Pitch picture for the end of each phrase.)

Mister Rooster and Mrs. Hen — NEIDLINGER, *Small Songs for Small Singers*, p. 9.

(Pitch pictures for the hen's and the rooster's calls.)

Whip-poor-will — OLDS, *Twenty-five Bird Songs*, p. 50.

(Pitch picture of the song.)

Three Little Kittens — CHEATHAM, *Nursery Garland*, p. 91.

(The teacher sings the verses and the children the chorus of which they make the pitch pictures.)

Scotland's burning — *Morning Stars Sang Together*, p. 217.

False Alarm — *Progressive Music Series, Teacher's Manual*, Vol. I, p. 212.

The Wind — SURETTE, *Rote Songs*, p. 16.

(Pitch picture of the cry of the wind which consists of the tones of the tonic chord.)

Frères Jacques — NEWMAN, *The Children's Own Book*, p. 13.

(Pitch pictures of din, din, don.)

Who Knocks? — *Progressive Music Series, Teacher's Manual*, Vol. I, p. 292.

The Bells — SURETTE, *Rote Songs*, p. 26.

(Pitch picture of the bells.)

Echo Song — SURETTE, *Rote Songs*, p. 34.

(Pitch picture of the echo.)

Elves' Dance — SURETTE, *Rote Songs*, p. 60.

(Pitch picture of the elves' dance.)

Songs are also created in the form of Question and Answer with Pitch Pictures made of the Answers. Thus:

The teacher sings:

What does   lit - tle   bird - ie   say?

The class answers:

" Peep, peep,   peep."

Making Pitch Pictures

© UNDERWOOD & UNDERWOOD
STUDIOS N. Y.

The following is the " Pitch Picture " as the children would write it:

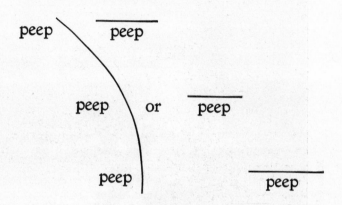

The following is a *List of Songs* preceded by an illustration in which the entire melody may be used for " Pitch Pictures," and for which the teacher asks the children to follow the direction of each melody with their hands and in writing, as they followed the course of the aeroplane:

ILLUSTRATION

WRITTEN PITCH PICTURE

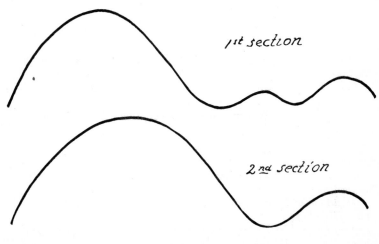

1st section

2nd section

SONGS*

Wise Old Owl:
  NEIDLINGER, *Small Songs for Small Singers*, p. 20.
The River:
  RILEY AND GAYNOR, *Songs of the Child-World*, p. 48.
Tiddlely-winks and Tiddlely-wee:
  NEIDLINGER, *Small Songs for Small Singers*, p. 19.
Mister Frog:
  NEIDLINGER, *Small Songs for Small Singers*, p. 28.
Playing Ball on the Stairs:
  SURETTE, *Rote Songs*, p. 36.
The Blue-bird:
  NEWMAN, *The Children's Own Book*, p. 26.
The Clown — (French folk-song):
  Progressive Music Series, Teacher's Manual, Vol. I, p. 206.
Happy Thought — (Old English Song):
  Progressive Music Series, Teacher's Manual, Vol. I, p. 219.
Sleigh Bells:
  Progressive Music Series, Teacher's Manual, Vol. I, p. 300.
Hymn of Praise — (Beethoven):
  NEWMAN, *The Children's Own Book*, p. 5.
The Hunter's Horn — (Beethoven):
  NEWMAN, *The Children's Own Book*, p. 23.

  * For very small children omit this list and substitute the songs in *The Children's Own Book*.

When Fields are White:
   SURETTE, *Rote Songs*, p. 9.
A Picnic on the Grass:
   SURETTE, *Rote Songs*, p. 11.
Robin:
   OLDS, *Twenty-five Bird Songs for Children*, p. 31.
Song Sparrow:
   OLDS, *Twenty-five Bird Songs for Children*, p. 40.

Nursery Rhyme Melodies

The Spider and the Fly:
   MOFFAT, *Little Songs of Long Ago*, p. 55.
Hey, Diddle, Diddle:
   NEWMAN, *The Children's Own Book*, p. 30.
Pussy-cat, pussy-cat:
   Most Popular Mother Goose Songs, p. 10.
I Love Little Pussy:
   Most Popular Mother Goose Songs, p. 19.
Dickery, Dickery, Dock:
   Most Popular Mother Goose Songs, p. 31.
Little Tom Tucker:
   MOFFAT, *Little Songs of Long Ago*, p. 51.

GAMES AND DRILLS FOR HEARING THE EXACT TONES IN SONGS

(To be used in connection with and as a preparation for the
Graded songs listed in Chapter XI. The number of tones used
for each game is the number necessary for each group of songs.)

GAME

BIRDS' NESTS

(CREATED BY MARJORIE DICE)

The teacher (or a pupil) draws a tree with as many branches as
tones to be considered, numbers them, and on each draws a bird's
nest.

She tells the children that each bird has a different tone (the
successive scale tones) and that, as the tone of any one is played,
each child, in turn, is to sing it by number-name and draw a straw
in the nest of the corresponding number. Any child failing to
sing a tone correctly loses his turn to draw. After the nests are
filled with straws, eggs are added.

This same idea is used in decorating a Christmas tree before the Christmas season, in filling sacks with apples before Thanksgiving, or nests with eggs before Easter, as well as the ringing of bells before New Year's.

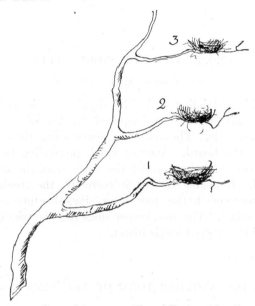

BLIND-MAN'S BUFF

The teacher blindfolds one child in the center of a circle formed by the rest of the class. All except the one in the center skip around while singing the following song:

Words by CECILIA VAN CLEVE*

In the ring we're skipping light-ly, Keep-ing out of blind-man's way.

Tell us, blind-man, can you right-ly Guess the tones that we will play?

* "Words from Folk-dances for Young People," by Cecilia Van Cleve, published by Milton Bradley Co.

When the song is ended, one child leaves the circle and plays on the piano one or more of the (scale) tones with which the children are familiar, which the blindfolded child is to recognize and sing by number-name, after which another is blindfolded and the game continues.

NO. I — GAME OF STOREKEEPER

(Created by Mildred Rider)

One child, pretending to be the storekeeper, is seated at the piano with his wares — the required number of scale-tones — all ready for sale. The numbers representing these tones are written on the board. Another child, pretending to be a customer, chooses and sings one of the tones from the numbers on the board. If unable to sing it correctly, the teacher assists. The customer goes to the storekeeper, sings this tone and asks to have it matched. The storekeeper sings it as he tries each of his tones until the desired one is found.

NO. II. — ANOTHER FORM OF THE SAME GAME

To Match Two, Three or More Tones

Another game of " Storekeeper " is played in which the desired numbers   3

2

1

are written on the board and the storekeeper asked to intone any one of the five black or seven white tones in the middle scale of the keyboard. The tone given is sung by the customer at the blackboard as 1, from which he sings the others 2 and 3. Then he goes to the storekeeper, sings them and asks to have them matched. In like manner, songs that include the same number of tones are bought, in which the customer asks the storekeeper to reproduce the melodies at the keyboard just as he sings them. He sings a pattern or a motif at a time.

GAME OF "MINE"

(CREATED BY MILDRED RIDER)

The children choose one tone of a song and call it "mine." The teacher plays the song, and each time the children hear the chosen tone, they sing "mine." The song or game is repeated until every tone has been chosen and sung to the same name.

MUSIC–BOX GAME OR THE CHIMES

Each child pretends to be one of the scale-tones in a Music-box or one of the bells of the Chimes, and the number of children chosen to represent these tones depends upon the number of scale-tones contained in the songs to be "played" or sung. As, for the list of songs containing three scale-tones, one child pretends to be 1, another 2, and another 3. Still another child pretending to be the "conductor" chooses a song and has the "music-box" or "chimes" sing it as he points or taps in rhythm for the required tones.

To make the game more interesting, the children try to discover the name of the song as they sing it.

A PITCH DRILL

The teacher writes the scale numbers on the board: ī

7

6

5

4

3

2

1̲

and tells the children that she will play short phrases composed of two or more of these numbers to which they are to sing and point as they hear. Then she plays short phrases like these:

1̲	2	1̲					1	3	4	2	1
1̲	2	3	1̲				1	2	4	2	1
1̲	3	1̲					1	2	3	4	5	1
1̲	2	3	4	3	2	1	1	3	5		l etc.

The " leap " home at the end of each phrase, and an irregular succession of tones familiarizes the children with the distance between tones, namely, Intervals.

" Pitch-Pictures " for the First Songs

(To be Expressed at the Keyboard as Listed in Chapter XI)

After the above games and drills have been given, it is no effort for the children to hear the separate tones of the songs as listed in Chapter XI, and to make the " Pitch Pictures." For the latter, a straight line for each separate tone has been found more useful than the continuous line for each phrase, as a greater demand is thereby made for listening for the quality of each tone, its placing in the scale, and its distance from the one preceding it. Each phrase is given a separate division.

ILLUSTRATIONS

I

Song of one phrase, with Pitch Picture:

II

Song of two phrases, with Pitch Picture:

ANOTHER PLAN FOR HEARING INTERVALS
(CREATED BY MILDRED RIDER)

It is assumed that the children are able to hear and play the "steps" and "slides" (as explained in Chapter X, The Scale), the distance between each, the teacher explains, is called an *Interval of a Second*. She also explains that a scale line is not always followed in songs, but that a "leap" is very frequently made from one tone over 1, — 2, — 3, — 4, — or more tones which, in Harmony, is called an *Interval*, but that, as a convenience for them it will be called a "leap." If one scale tone is passed, the result is a "leap" or "*Interval of a third*"; 2 tones, an *Interval of a fourth;* 3 tones, an *Interval of a fifth*, and so on. The children must become gradually familiar with intervals as they hear them in the songs while making the "Pitch Pictures" with their hands, or in writing as they fill in the distance between the "Pitch Picture" lines.* As for illustration, the first phrase of the song, "Cuckoo."

Cuck - oo, cuck - oo, Calls from the wood.

PITCH PICTURE

DIRECTIONS

The teacher or one child in the class sings the first two tones of the song:

Cuck-

−oo

---

* The teacher should have this subject very clear in her own mind so as to avoid any confusion in explaining it. It is not intended for very small children.

after which the rest of the class fill in the distance between by
singing the scale tones 5, 4, 3, to discover the name of the Interval
between the two tones.   This is found to be an Interval of a Third
and is added to the written " Pitch Picture."

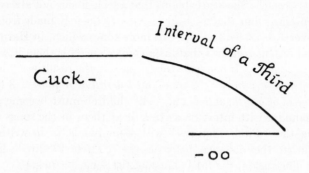

Again the class sings the scale-tones of the Interval, but this
time, listens to be able to name each as a " step " or " slide," in
order to discover the exact distance between the two tones; as,
(5) " step," " slide."   This is also added to the " Pitch " lines.

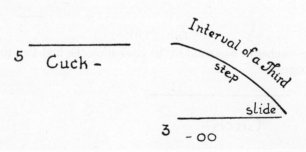

The same plan is followed for discovering the names of all of
the other Intervals of the song and the exact distance between
them.

CHAPTER IX

NOTATION

For this subject the teacher uses her ingenuity and imagination to the utmost; for the interest in it to be awakened within the minds of the children depends entirely upon the way in which it is presented.

Notation is apt to be a danger point in the progress of musical development as it is easy for the teacher to become too quickly involved in technical and complicated details of note values.

The creative teacher makes this a special study, consulting the Reference Departments of the best libraries for material on the Evolution of Music. Thus sufficiently equipped, she is able to tell the children, in the *simplest form*, stories regarding the origin of music and its gradual development from the earliest known sources to the present time. This would include stories about the expression of the emotions of the primitive races by means of song and the first crude instruments they developed to give them outside expression; the gradual discovery and development of the science of tone; the evolution of musical instruments; and finally, the expression of these thoughts and songs by means of writing. She emphasizes the necessity of writing music, not only because it is the only exact method of preserving it in every period of time, but also because it is the medium by means of which music may be instantly read or sung without the aid of the musical instrument for which it was intended, and, later, expressed at the keyboard as it was heard without the written notes as a guide.

To equip children for this important work is one of the main objects of this book; and to this end, the teacher uses her own judgment in not presenting too much of this subject at a time.

She illustrates the staff of two or three lines and spaces which represented the form used in the 12th and 13th centuries, and traces its gradual evolution through many changes, including forms from four to twenty-five lines until it developed into the staff of five lines and four spaces that is recognized to-day.

The children draw it:

Lines ⁵⁄₄⅜²⁄₁ ═══════════════════════════ ⁴⁄₃²⁄₁ Spaces

She tells them that it was found to be so convenient that it gradually came to be adopted to the exclusion of all others, and that in order to simplify the writing and give the necessary spacing for notes, as the musical consciousness developed, " *leger lines* " were invented and added above and below the staff.

Also, that for piano music two staffs became necessary, one for the treble notes, the other for the bass notes.

For the treble notes

For the bass notes

that they were connected by a brace,

and that each became designated by a different clef.

She then tells them something of the evolution of the Clefs; that they were first used to alter the names of the lines when the staffs consisted of only two, three or four lines and the compass of a melody overlapped the given spacing; and that, since then they have varied considerably both as to form and method of use.

That the *F* or *Bass Clef* is now always drawn around the fourth line of the lower staff and is the oldest of the clefs, having been the one used when the staffs consisted of but a single line.

That the *G* or *Treble Clef* placed on the upper staff — the lower part of which is drawn about the *G* line — came into general use when instrumental music rose to importance during the 16th and 17th centuries.

She asks them to draw these *Clefs* — the G on the upper staff, the F on the lower — and at the same time to consider the names of the lines about which they are drawn, in order to form a clear mental picture of their positions.

Also to consider these two staffs together as the "*Grand Staff*" upon which the notes are to be written.

She illustrates the order in which the notes are written on the "Grand Staff" by beginning with "Middle C" on the first leger line below the treble staff, and the first above the bass staff, and writing them in successive order for both ascending and descending. She does the same with the notes for the *leger lines*.

The children are not asked to remember the notes at this time, as the object of this explanation is merely to acquaint them with the order in which they are written.

ILLUSTRATION

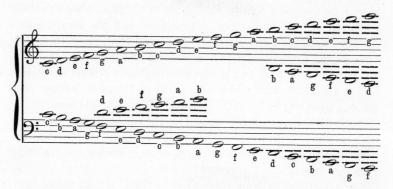

In order to familiarize the children with the keyboard and the written notes more or less unconsciously, several plans and games have been evolved. The creative teacher, however, will devise her own.

Introduction of the Notes by Means of Visualization

Now the teacher explains that the notes are given names by which they are identified, just as children are given names, and that each has a place on the keyboard and on the staff. After they have become familiar with them they will be able to play their first " note-game."

They are also told that all of the notes of one letter-name are considered relatives; as, for illustration; all of the C's that are written upon the Treble and Bass staffs. And then they are introduced to " Middle C's " place at the keyboard and to its two places on the staff.

The teacher then asks them to close their eyes and form a picture of them in their minds. She then tells them the Middle C has two cousins, one of whom lives a block above, and the other a block below, and illustrates their positions both at the keyboard and at the staff.

In order to aid them in forming a clear mental picture of these notes, she asks them to compare their positions. They notice that one is located on the second space from the top in the treble-staff and the other on the second space from the bottom in the bass-staff, after which they close their eyes and see them mentally.*

This same plan is followed for the six remaining letter-names to include all of the notes on the treble and the bass staffs.†

GAME

A Note Party

(CREATED BY MILDRED RIDER)

The teacher draws a Grand Staff on the board and tells the children they are to have a Note Party, and that the individual tones are to be invited by the ringing of their door-bells; that is, by the striking of their tones, after which they are to be given their seats at the party; meaning their places on the Grand Staff; as:

The Invitation and Arrival of the C's

One child rings Middle C's door-bell and seats her at the party — (draws her two places on the Grand Staff), then rings Middle C's two cousins' bells, who live a block above and below Middle C's

---

* Whenever a comparison or association of notes is possible, it is advisable to use it as the children are thereby enabled to visualize more readily and the mental pictures are more pronounced.

† The advantage of this plan and the following game is that the children become familiar with the exact position of the notes without the usual preliminary spelling that has been the custom more or less in the past.

home, and gives them their respective places. Another child, in the same manner, invites the G's; another the F's and so on, until all of the notes having places on the treble and bass staffs have been included.

When all of the tones have been given their places, the game is prolonged by returning them to their homes. This is done by each child in turn, checking or erasing a note as it is supposed to leave and ringing the door-bell (striking its note) to signify the return home.

The following is the final result of the game:

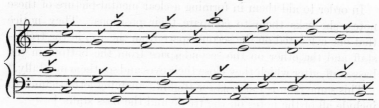

GAME

Sight-Singing for Notation

(CREATED BY MARJORIE DICE)

In a small music blank-book the teacher writes the notes of a very simple, original melody for each page. For the first game, she writes them for melodies in which only two tones of the scale are used, as:

She intones " Middle C " and asks each child in turn:

First. — To open the tablet at random and to sing by sight and by letter-name the melody on the particular page.

Second. — To play the notes as they have been sung.

The child wins who has sung and played the greatest number correctly.

For the next game, or after they have become familiar with those two tones and notes, another scale-tone is added to those previously used, as:

Then melodies containing these three and another,

and so on as long as the interest of the children is maintained.

After each game the children are eager to make up melodies of their own containing the notes that were sung, which they, in turn, write on the board, and the teacher further specifies a certain number for them to " make up " and write for home-work.

The object of this game is to give the children an opportunity to become more familiar with the notes on the staff and on the piano.

The children are now prepared to sing by sight the songs that have been carefully chosen for beginners and are, to their great delight, introduced to their First Reader, " The Children's Own Book." This is developed simply and gradually for the melody, rhythm, and harmony.

Directions for the Application of Each Song in the Reader

After the children have sung the scale in which a song is written and the song by letter-names to the correct tones while fingering it away from the piano, the teacher asks them:

1. To sing the words of the song while swinging the rhythm.*

2. To sing the song as they swing, in phrases and with expression.

3. To express it at the keyboard with the same expression and feeling with which it was sung.

* If they are unable to do this, the teacher refers to the drills given in Chapter III, "Directions for Discovering Time," and Chapter IV, "Rhythmic Notation," and applies them to the present needs.

4. To sing the song in rhythm to the scale numbers, provided they have completed the games and drills in Chapter VII — " The Scale " — and are able to hear the exact distance between the tones.

5. For each child in turn, to play the song with a feeling of expression and rhythm — each song in a different key which is designated by the teacher.

6. To sing the simple chords under the melody according to the directions given in Chapter X — " Harmony " — and to write a chord pattern.

7. For each child to play the chord pattern in a different key as the rest of the class sings.

8. To play the song, both melody and the simple chords in any key, with feeling and rhythm.

9. For home-work, the teacher asks the children to write both the melody and the chords in several keys.

FRENCH SYSTEM OF NOTATION

The French System of Notation is used in this work as it has been found to save time in writing, and is particularly convenient for dictation. It consists of oblique lines instead of notes, as,

which are later changed into the required note values, for which see " Rhythmic Notation," in Chapter IV, " Melodic Dictation," this chapter, and " Directions," in Chapter XI, " First Songs for the Children to Play."

SCALE NOTATION — MAJOR AND MINOR

(*A Continuation of Paragraph 10, Chapter VII, p. 56*)

After the children are perfectly familiar with the scales by having sung them to letters and fingered them, the teacher asks them to write them in their blank music-books while singing them to the letter-names; to write them up on the treble-staff, and down on the bass-staff twice, the first time placing the sharps or flats in front of the notes to which they belong (in order to become

familiar with the written notes), and the second time to write the
signatures in their proper places on the staff (for practice in writing
the signatures correctly). She then asks them to write them in
their final rhythmic form according to the directions given in
Chapter VII, Paragraph 4.

The regular order for their succession, as indicated by the circle
of keys, is followed. The examples below are illustrations of the
forms in which they are written.

MINOR

(A Continuation of "The Minor Scale," Chapter VII)

The same plan for the Major Scale Notation is followed for the
Notation of the three related Minor Scales except that the first
two forms are omitted, since the children are in all probability
familiar with the notes at this time and the third or Rhythmic
Form is used immediately.

The following is an illustration of the first Major and its related
minors to be written.

C, MAJOR

A, NATURAL MINOR

A, HARMONIC MINOR

A, MELODIC MINOR

Melodic and Harmonic Dictation

The following is the simplest form of dictation that has been used most successfully for small children and is given after they have a consciousness of the scale, are familiar with the separate scale-tones from the "Pitch Games," and are able to hear the distances between "steps," "slides" and "leaps."

A folk-song may be selected that has been developed according to the directions contained in Numbers 1 to 18 in Chapter XI, " The First Songs for the Children to Play."

Directions for Melodic Dictation

In their blank music books the children connect two staffs with a brace, write the Treble and Bass Clefs in their respective places, choose a line or space on which to write the first tone, and become very quiet in order to listen attentively to every tone the teacher plays. (A staff is always reserved for the bass note accompaniment.)

As an illustration, the first phrase (which is complete) of the folk-song " Hum, hum, hum," is used, and it will be supposed that the children have chosen the third line of the staff on which to begin to write.

Hum, hum, hum, Hap - py lit - tle top, When I loose the
string that bound you, Songs come spin - ning all a - round you.
Hum, hum, hum, Hap - py lit - tle top.

The first phrase of the song — beginning on the line chosen by the children — is:

Hum, hum, hum, Hap - py lit - tle top.

The teacher plays the song for the children to sing the home-tone and establish a feeling of the scale consciousness of this particular key. Then she plays the first tone after which she stops and asks the first child to sing it by scale-tone number. (In this song the first tone is the fifth scale number from which point the other numbers proceed forward and backward.)

After it is sung correctly by the first child, it is written by the class (according to the French System of Notation and according to the following directions) as the number-name is sung.

The teacher plays the second tone and asks the next child to sing its scale-tone number (which is 4) after which it is written by the class in the second space as the number-name is sung. And so on with all the other tones of the song until the final result of the dictation is:

The teacher then asks the class:

1. To sing the home-tone, name the key in which the song has been written, sing or write the scale, and add the key-signature to both the Treble and the Bass staffs.

2. To sing the written notes by letter-names.

3. To add the bar lines as they sing and swing, change the oblique lines into their proper note-values, and complete the song rhythmically according to the directions given in this chapter for French System of Notation, and Directions 10 to 18 in Chapter XI, " The First Songs for the Children to Play."

The result is:

Directions for Harmonic Dictation

1. The teacher plays the song and asks the children while swinging to sing the chords underneath the melody.

2. To write them as they swing (with the left hand) and sing.

3. To write the fundamental chord notes while singing the numbers.

4. To write the two remaining tones of each chord while singing their numbers, 3 and 5, after repeating the first, as:

5. To sing the letter names of the chord tones.

6. To change the oblique lines into the proper note values.

For further details, see " Harmony," next chapter.

CHAPTER X

HARMONY

From harmony, from heavenly harmony
This universal frame began;
When Nature underneath a heap
Of jarring atoms lay,
And could not heave her head,
The tuneful voice was heard from high,
"Arise, ye more than dead!"
Then cold and hot, and moist and dry,
In order to their stations leap,
And Music's power obey.
From harmony, from heavenly harmony, ·
This universal frame began;
From harmony to harmony
Through all the compass of the notes it ran,
The diapason closing full in Man. — DRYDEN.

In the past, Harmony has too often been considered a technical
and academic subject, and, therefore, too difficult for children.
To the average student of music theory it has frequently come to
mean blank-books filled with notes and numbers seldom heard or
applied at the keyboard.   The idea seems to have prevailed that
it is necessary to be born with the faculty for hearing especially
well developed if one is to successfully harmonize melodies " by
ear."

The progressive modern teachers, however, go to work upon the basis that the ability to play melodies and harmonize them by ear, is a fundamental background for all music study, and that unless children are taught to pick out melodies and harmonize them in this way, their music lessons become mechanical and almost inevitably boring.

Recently it is becoming more generally known that the faculty for hearing harmonies and melodies can be developed in children who are themselves unable to sing, provided they be started at the work at a sufficiently early age. Even later these results are obtained if the student will give enough time and application to the task.

The special training of the faculty for hearing melodies and their underlying harmonies is a splendid means of catching and holding the interest of children who ordinarily would not be musically inclined. It develops concentration to a marked degree. Teachers are frequently amazed to see the results after a year or two of study, when their pupils will play for them accompaniments to songs that have not been learned in class and demonstrate the ability to harmonize melodies of school songs in any key freely and rhythmically.

As Melody and Harmony are very closely related, Harmony should be introduced *in connection* with Melody, that the child may realize from the beginning the effect and use of the principal chords in the musical scheme.

These are introduced very gradually, and the children should be led to *listen* and *hear* the tones of which the chords are composed before they *spell* (sing these tones by number and letter-names), *write* and *play* them.

The first chord introduced is the Tonic (I), and songs are sung and played in which this one chord can be used to harmonize the entire melody.

Then the *Dominant* (V) and *Dominant-seventh* (V₇), are introduced. Melodies are chosen that can be harmonized with these chords. The same procedure is followed with the *Subdominant* (IV) *chord*.

After the children have become perfectly familiar with these, which comprise the Major chords of the scale, and after they are able to *number*, *write* and *play* them, the corresponding *Minor chords* of the scale, i.e., the *Supertonic* (ii), *Sub-mediant* (vi), and *Mediant* (iii), are gradually presented and the same plan followed for their harmonization.*

According to the plan given above, the melodies to be harmonized with these chords are listed and graded in the required order in Chapter XI, " First Songs for the Children to Play," with, however, one exception; that the list begins with songs to be harmonized with the I and V or V₇ chords, while the melodies over the Tonic chord alone are mentioned in this, Chapter X. Original melodies which can be harmonized with these fundamental chords are desirable along with the songs, already mentioned.

Thus by a slow process of growth is the faculty of hearing harmonically developed. The result is a foundation indispensable to musicians. It simplifies memorizing which resolves itself into nothing more than hearing correctly, and not the mere remembering of notes.

It makes Improvisation and Transposition possible; the harmonization of any song that is inwardly heard becomes a natural and simple matter, and the ability to express original musical ideas is spontaneously developed.

Only general directions necessary for the Class work can be given in this treatise together with the attempt to make them so clear and simple, that students without a knowledge of harmony will be enabled to apply them.

It is assumed, however, that every teacher of this method has or will make an intensive study of Harmony, in order to assist the children in the harmonic analysis and transposition of every composition that is given in their private instruction as they advance musically.

---

* The order followed for the Minor chords in this volume, is due to the frequency of these chords in the folk-songs and dances. All Minor chords are indicated by smaller numerals than are used for Major chords.

For Recognizing a Chord and Its Root or " Home-tone "

1. The teacher tells the children something about chords, for illustration, that they are played underneath a melody to enrich it, and that they consist of several concordant tones; i.e., tones which have an agreeable sound when played together and that they are as effective musically as beautiful colors when harmonized in a painting.

To explain this a Tonic chord is played

and the pupils are asked to listen and tell the number of tones of which it is composed. If they are unable to do this, the chord is played three times, and each time one of its three separate tones is brought out more forcibly than the others by means of the pedal and a greater pressure of the key.

After they discover that the chord is made up of three tones, this process is repeated, and they are asked to listen again in order to tell whether one tone gives more of a feeling of " rest " or " home " than the others.

When this tone is recognized, they sing it to the syllable " la." This is repeated in all of the other keys and continued until they are able to hear and sing the " home-tones " of the Tonic or I chord in any key without any uncertainty.

Naming the I Chord

2. The teacher plays a Tonic chord; then plays the scale to which that chord belongs and asks if there is any difference in feeling in the " resting " or " home-tone " of the chord and the scale. When they realize that the " home-tones " of both are the same and that they are on the first tone of the scale, the teacher tells them that the chord is given the name of " one " or Tonic, and will be represented by the Roman numeral, I.

The playing of the Tonic chord is repeated in all keys, and the children sing the " home-tone," but this time to the name of *one* (I) instead of " la."

The Application of the I or Tonic Chord

3. The following is a group of songs under which the I chord may be sung throughout and which are used in the beginning to give the children the first feeling of a harmonized tone beneath the melody.

SUNSHINE BRIGHT

In " The Children's Own Book "

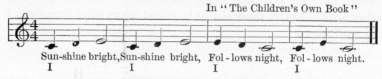

Sun-shine bright, Sun-shine bright, Fol-lows night, Fol-lows night.
I   I   I   I

THE RHINE MOTIVE

In " The Children's Own Book "

I   I   I   I

FRÈRE JACQUES

In " The Children's Own Book "

I   I   I

Frè - re Jac - ques, Frè - re Jac - ques, dor - mez - vous,

I   I

dor - mez - vous?   Son - nez les ma - ti - nes,

I

Son - nez les ma - ti - nes, Din, din, don! Din, din, don!

BUGLE CALL

In " The Children's Own Book "

I   I   I   I

I   I   I   I

If the melodies of the last three are too difficult for performance at the keyboard when used for this purpose, the chords are played as a harmonic basis without the melody, after they have been sung and written. But the first, " Sunshine Bright," is one of the first melodies for the children to play, and consequently may be expressed both melodically and harmonically in all keys. The teacher plays these songs for the children to sing and swing, after which they sing the " home-tone " of the I chord in the key in which it has been played. As these songs are repeated, the children are asked as they swing, to sing this *chord-tone* " one " (I) each time the swing changes and to listen attentively to determine whether it harmonizes each time with the melodies.

(At the words " din, din, don," in Frère Jacques, the melody is sung and the harmony omitted.

For Writing the Chord Patterns

4. As the songs are repeated in the above manner, the teacher asks one child to go to the board and write this chord number, I, each time it is sung by the class, and to begin each phrase on a separate line. The results are:

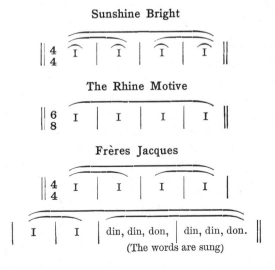

Sunshine Bright

The Rhine Motive

Frères Jacques

(The words are sung)

Bugle Call

$$\left\| \begin{array}{c} 4 \\ 4 \end{array} \right| \text{I} \mid \text{I} \mid \text{I} \mid \text{I} \mid$$

$$\mid \text{I} \mid \text{I} \mid \quad \mid \text{I} \mid \|$$

For Singing the Root or "Home-tone" of the Tonic Chord with the Melodies

ORCHESTRA GAME

(CREATED BY MILDRED RIDER)

5. The children pretend to play orchestra. One child is chosen as conductor, the rest of the class being separated into two divisions, one of which pretends to play solo instruments — such as the violin — while singing the song; and the other the accompaniments or bass instruments — like the Double-Bass — while singing the roots of the chords. The conductor's duty is to swing the rhythm and keep the players together. Each pretended stroke of the bow on the instruments is to represent a swing or measure, and the *chord patterns* on the board may be followed by the side that is playing the accompaniments.

For the children to sing together successfully, much practice in the separate parts is necessary; and when the " full " orchestra plays and sings, the teacher assists the weaker side.

For Playing the Root or "Home-tone" of the I Chord as the Melodies are Sung, when the Game is Repeated

6. The teacher asks one child to go to the piano and play the root or " home-tone " of the chord as it is sung and played by the Bass instruments, and, if the melodic work for these three songs has been completed, she asks another, at the same time, to play the melody as it is sung and played by the solo instruments. This adds to the interest of the game.

For Writing the Root or "Home-tone" of the I Chord

7. The teacher asks the children to turn to those melodies that had been written in their blank music-books, and, under the Bass staffs (which have been reserved) and immediately after each

Playing " Orchestra "

bar line (since each bar line represents the beginning of a swing), to write the chord-names as they were written in the chord-patterns. While they write, the teacher plays the melodies to assist them in writing them rhythmically, and they sing the chords by name, as:

Sunshine Bright

I   I   I   I

The same with the other three melodies under which the I chord is heard.

They write the root-note of the I chord (which they readily discover, since it is the same as the keynote) on the bass-staff while singing it to the letter-name, thus:

Sunshine Bright

I   I   I   I

For Hearing the Three Tones of the I Chord

8. The class, previously led to realize that a chord is made up of three harmonious tones, is now to be assisted in hearing them, after which they are to sing, play and write them in all keys. To command their attention and to get them in a listening attitude, the teacher makes up stories of which the following are illustrations:

STORY I

The teacher plays the first five tones of any scale and tells the pupils that these are supposed to be five children, all of whom live next door to one another in the same block; that the child in the first house (she plays her tone, the first of the scale) went to the park with her nurse every day, but was very lonely and longed for two congenial playmates. The nurse, hearing of the children in the same block, decided to give each a separate trial until two such playmates were found. She invites the child who lives next door. The teacher plays this second scale-tone with the first, and asks the class if they think she is one of the children the nurse is seeking. At the sound of the discord produced, they agree she is not. The nurse invites the child at the third house, and when the children hear this third tone played with the first, they feel certain that the first playmate has been found. Rejection of the fourth tone follows when played with 1 and 3; but when 5 is reached, the other playmate — the child in the 5th house — is chosen and invited.

STORY II

The same idea as the one in the story above is used in pretending to try five bells in an effort to find three which, when rung together, will produce a beautiful and harmonious sound.

For Singing the Three Chord-tones

9. The three tones, the 1, 3 and 5, are sung separately by the children and a " Spelling-match game " played (explained in Chapter VII, " The Scale ") in which a different keynote is introduced at each repetition.

For Playing the Three Chord Tones

10. The teacher asks each child in turn, to go to the keyboard and sing and play the separate notes of the chord, after introducing a keynote on any of the black or white keys. Then to combine the three tones and listen for the effect they produce. (Very small children are able to play only two of the chord tones at one time.)

For Writing the Three Chord-tones

11. The class is asked to translate the chord numbers 3 and 5 into notes in the key in which the fundamental chord-tones have already been written underneath melodies in their blank music-

books (see Direction 7, this Chapter), and to add them above the fundamental notes while singing them to letter-names. Illustration:

Sunshine Bright

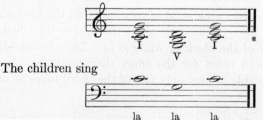

For Playing the Song, both Melody and Harmony

12. The teacher chooses one child to play the melody, another the full chords, another to write the chord-pattern on the board while singing the notes as they are played, and the remaining members of the class to sing and swing the melody. (At each repetition the key is changed.) She asks each child in turn (and each time in a different key) to play both melody and chords.

THE DOMINANT V CHORD

(a) For Hearing the Dominant V Chord

13. The teacher repeats the process of playing the I Chord for the children to sing the " root-tone," but this time adds the *V Chord* with its root at the bass. The children now sing both " root-tones " to the syllable " la," as:

The teacher plays

The children sing

This is played and sung in all keys.

* This chord connection contrary to the rules of Harmony is introduced and applied before the closely related positions, so the children can become familiar with the formation of the chords from their Root tones.

One child playing the chords as they are sung and written by a child at the black-board—another playing the melody as it is sung and swung by the rest of the class.

The children are asked if they remember any part of a song they have recently sung with the same melody as these connected chords. They recall " din, din, don," in " Frères Jacques," which will later prove invaluable in finding these " root-tones " quickly and in any key.

(b) For Naming the V Chord

The class is asked if they recognize the scale number of the *root* or " home-tone " of this middle chord, if not, to sing the scale backwards by number until the desired tone is reached. They sing (two octaves higher than they write).

8   7   6   5

When they associate this tone with the fifth tone of the scale, it is explained, by a written illustration, that this chord is built upon the fifth tone of the scale in the same manner as the I chord which was built upon the first, namely:

8   7   6   5

Also, that it is given the name of " Five " or " Dominant " and represented by the Roman numeral V.

As the teacher plays these chords in all keys, the children sing the " roots " to the chord names, as:

One, (I) — Five (V) — One (I).
or
Tonic — Dominant — Tonic

(c) The Application of the Dominant V Chord

The songs that are to be harmonized with this chord are listed in Chapter XI (first part of list), " The First Songs for the Children to Play," and are graded accordingly. The " close " positions are used, however, as soon as they are heard. (See directions 18, this Chapter, for " close " positions.) The Dominant-seventh (V_7) is also to be included, but only after the children have become thoroughly familiar with the Dominant (V). For very small children the V is sufficient. The V₇ chord is explained later.

The teacher plays a song given in the list, as " Cuckoo " (" The Children's Own Book "), and asks the children to sing one of the two chords — the I or the V under each measure (or swing) of the melody. To do this it is necessary for them to listen very attentively, and, occasionally, try both chords until the one that harmonizes is found.

(d) For Writing the Chord-Pattern

CHORD PATTERN FOR "CUCKOO"

(The same as Direction 4, this Chapter)

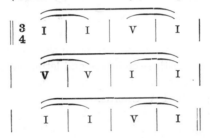

(e) For Singing the Root of the Dominant (V) Chord with the Melody

(Same as Direction 5 in this Chapter)

The " Orchestra Game " may be used throughout the chord work. It will become more effective and helpful as time goes on, and when the " bass musicians " are able to hear more of the harmonic changes.

(f) For Playing the " Roots " of the Chords from the Chord-Pattern as the Melodies are Sung

To find the " root-tone " of the V chord quickly after the first tone of the I chord is heard in any key, the children listen for the tones to agree with the familiar " din, din, don " from the song " Frères Jacques," or to agree with the interval of the fourth, downward (I V I) as it had been sung in all keys before it is applied to the given melodies.

(g) For Writing the Root-notes of the V Chord

The note representing the Dominant chord is readily found by writing (while singing) the scale backwards, both by number and letter-name, on the bass-staff, after the key-note or root-tone of the I chord is written, as:

1 or 8   7   6   5

or by hearing the interval of the fourth and being able to measure the distance accordingly.

c   g   c
I   V   I

The teacher asks the children to write the root-notes of I, V, I, as they sing them to these numbers and letter-names in all of the keys before the notes are written under the first melodies to be harmonized with the I–V–Chords.

The same directions are then followed as those given for the I chord and explained in Direction 7, in this Chapter.

The following is an illustration of the song " Cuckoo."

CUCKOO

German Folk-Tune

Cuck - oo, cuck - oo, Calls from the wood; Let us be sing - ing,

I   I   V   I   V   V

danc- ing, and spring-ing, Spring-time, spring-time, Soon will be here.

I   I   I   I   V   I

(h) For Hearing, Singing, Playing and Writing the Separate Tones of the V Chord

For the V chord and also for the IV chord (Subdominant) the same directions are followed as those given in 8, 9 and 10 of this Chapter. However, if the preparation has been thorough, the children are at this time able to *hear, write* and *play* the two tones above the root-tones of these chords without further preliminary help.

The simplicity of this plan has been evolved by Mr. Frederick Schlieder, who has reduced the numbering for both the Major and Minor chords to simply 1, 3 and 5

If the chord-tones above the fundamental tone, that is to say, the 3 and 5 of the chord, are heard and recognized in the Major chord of a scale, they can be readily recognized in the Major chords of every scale, since the intervals are identical. So the only special preparation necessary after the separate tones of the I chord have been heard, is the *hearing, singing, writing* and *playing* of the " root-tones " of the V and IV chords.

Here is an illustration of the formation of the Major chords of a Major Scale:

The same applies to the chord-tones, 3 and 5 of all the **Minor** chords. When they are sung in one Minor chord, they can be readily sung and heard in all.

The II, VI and III comprise the Minor chords of a Major Scale, and the following is an illustration of their formation in the key of C.

These *chord numbers* are not to be confounded with *scale numbers*, as they pertain to the chords alone, but the simplicity of the numbering has made this plan most applicable for children, and the result is a *chord consciousness* as distinct from *scale consciousness*.

The same directions are then followed as those given in No. 11 of this Chapter, for completing the chords under the songs in which the root-notes only have been written, as the illustration shows in Direction (g) of this Chapter.

1. For playing the above melody, see Directions No. 12, this Chapter.

The Dominant Seventh (V₇) Chord

14. This chord is not usually given to very small children as the V is sufficient to answer their needs. It is introduced to the older ones (about the age of eight), after much practice has been given in the hearing and application of the Dominant.

DIRECTIONS

The teacher plays the V₇ chord between the I or Tonic· both chords in the root positions, as:

The children are asked to listen and tell how it differs from the Dominant (V) and to explain the feeling it gives. If necessary, the added tone (which is the 7th from the Root) is struck more forcibly, and the children asked to sing it and the tone to which it must move before a quality of rest is given. The above (I V₇ I) is played in every key, giving the pupils an opportunity to sing the root-tones, and, at the same time, become familiar with the full V₇ chord as it is played in connection with the I chord.

As the teacher intones the keynote of any scale (which she changes at each repetition), she asks each child to sing from that tone the root-tones of the I V₇ I chords without further assistance from the keyboard; and, finally, the separate tones of each chord to the chord numbers. The following would be the result in the key of C.

Next, the same is written and played in various keys.

This V₇ chord is used for harmonization in the first list of songs given in Chapter XI, under " Songs to be Harmonized with the I, V and V₇ Chords." For its use and development with melodies, the same directions as those for the V chord are applicable.

Singing the Chord Roots Above the Tonic

15. So far, the IV, V and V₇ chord roots have been played and sung below the I chord, that the tones might not conflict with the tones of the melody under which they were sung and played, as,

Now these chords are to be played, sung, and heard in their " close " positions as well, thus:

for which it is necessary to hear and sing the root-tones of the chords above that of the I chord.

To hear the *root-tone* of the V and V₇ chords above the *root-tone* of the I chord, and also each separate scale-tone when used as a *root-tone* of its respective chord, another simple plan is to divide the scale into its two Tetrachords,

1st Tetrachord   2nd Tetrachord

and the class into two sections.   Each section is asked to alternate in the singing of a Tetrachord to the above rhythm, using scale-numbers, 1–2–3–4–, and 5–6–7–8–.   These groups should be sung quite rapidly and with many continuous repetitions.

The first Tetrachord is then reversed, thus:

1st Tetrachord reversed, 2nd Tetrachord

and the process repeated until the two Tetrachords, in their latter form, together become a most familiar melody to the children.

Directions for Singing the Roots of the I–V–IV–II–VI– and III Chords above the "Home-tone"

While the *Tetrachord Melody* is prominent in the children's minds, each one, in succession, is asked for one of its separate tones, and in the order in which the chords are generally used, as:

I	IV	V			
I	IV	II	V	I	
I	VI	IV	II	V	I
I	IV	III	VI	V	I, etc.

and the pupils sing the roots of the chords from the tones as they hear them in the Tetrachord melody.   This is always repeated before each new chord is introduced, so that the children will become familiar with its *root-tone* and be able to recognize its quality before it is sung under the melodies to be harmonized. Accenting the new chord root as the Tetrachord melody is sung, will also emphasize its quality.

The I Chord in Its Three Positions*

16. By this time the interest of the class is usually so awakened and their desire so great for increasing the beauty of harmonization, that no new games nor stories seem necessary. The following simple plan has proven practical.

(*a*) For hearing the root or " home-tone " in the three positions of the I chord.

The teacher plays the three positions of the I chord, as,

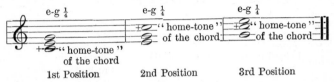

1st Position   2nd Position   3rd Position

and after each one, stops to ask the children to listen and sing the root or " home-tone." She continues to question, by suggestion and by greater intonation of the root-tone, until they discover for themselves that the three chords have the same root-tone, even though it is heard an octave higher in the second and third positions. She repeats this, each time playing the three positions out of their regular order, until the children are able to place and sing the root or " home-tone " of each without any hesitation. The same procedure is followed in all keys.

(*b*) For naming the three positions of the I chord and hearing the third and fifth chord-tones in each.

The teacher plays the I chord in its three positions:

and after each, asks the children to sing the " root-tone " and the other two tones, the third and the fifth, in the order of their placing in the chords. They continue listening and singing these tones

* The word "position" will be used through this chapter on Harmony in preference to the customary Harmonic term "inversion" because it has proven less confusing and simpler in dealing with children. In other words, a chord with the root at the bass, is said to be in the first position; the first inversion (third at bass) will be known as second position; the second inversion (fifth at bass) will be known as third position.

until they discover that they are the same in each of the chords played and that the only difference is in their arrangement, namely, that in the first chord, the root or " home-tone " or I is heard at the bottom and the fifth on top; in the second chord, the 3 (or third chord-tone) is heard at the bottom and the I on top; and in the third chord, the fifth is heard at the bottom, the root or " home-tone " in the middle, and the third on top.

She then explains that these chords are called respectively, the I chord in the first, second and third positions.

I chord in the   I chord in the   I chord in the
1st Position   2nd Position   3rd Position

DRILL

The teacher plays any one of these chords out of the regular order (in the same key for each lesson) and asks each child, separately, to sing the three tones of which each is composed in the order of their chord-numbers, and to name the position. The following is an illustration in the third position.

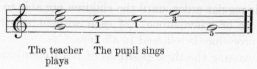

I
The teacher   The pupil sings
plays

(c) The children are given exercises for chord dictation in their blank music-books, following this example, second position:

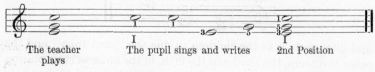

I
The teacher   The pupil sings and writes   2nd Position
plays

(d) The teacher asks each child, in turn, to play for the rest of the class to sing and write.

The V and V₇ Chords in Their Three Positions

17. (a) For hearing the three separate tones of the V chord in the three positions:

The teacher plays a Tonic chord in any key and asks the children to sing its " home-tone," and the root or " home-tone " of the V chord above the Tonic, according to the directions given in 15, this Chapter. The same plan is then followed as that given for the I chord (direction 16), in assisting the children to hear, write and play the separate tones and to name the positions, both for this chord and for the IV (Subdominant, explained in direction 19). The children will be able to do this immediately as IV is also a *Major Chord* and the same intervals lie between the tones of each of their positions.

Illustration of the three positions of the V chord as they are given:

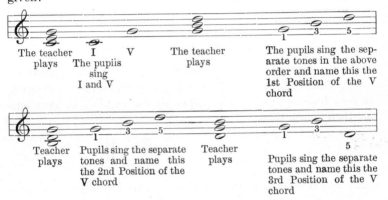

The teacher   I   V   The teacher   The pupils sing the sep-
plays   The pupils   plays   arate tones in the above
      sing   order and name this the
   I and V   1st Position of the V
                                                    chord

Teacher   Pupils sing the separate   Teacher   Pupils sing the separate
plays   tones and name this   plays   tones and name this the
         the 2nd Position of the   3rd Position of the V
         V chord   chord

(b) For hearing the three separate tones of the V_7 chord in the three positions:

The same directions as given for the V chord (17a) are followed for the V_7 chord in which case the 7th tone is added to the Dominant.

V V_7

The fifth tone of the chord is usually omitted, and the three positions found as the result of this omission are used for " close positions " with other chords.*

* Since we are omitting the fifth of the V_7 chord for the convenience of the child, we also omit, for the present, the third position (fifth at the bass, harmonically called second inversion of this V_7 chord).

Illustration for singing the three separate tones and for naming the positions:

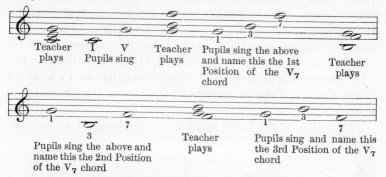

" Near " or " Close " Positions

18. Connecting the I and V and V₇ chords in " close " positions.

(a) The teacher plays the I V I chords, both in the first position, as they had been previously played by the children in harmonizing their songs, thus,

after which she plays the I as played, with the nearest position

of the V and asks the children which they prefer. They usually choose the " close position."

They are asked to sing the root and the separate tones of each in the order of the chord-numbers and to name the positions as they are played. The following is the result:

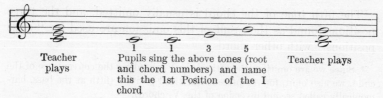

Pupils sing the above tones and name this the 2nd Position of the V chord

Teacher plays

Pupils sing

This is repeated in all keys.

(b) The same is played for chord dictation in the blank music-books, but this time in the order designated by the circle of keys. After each change of key, the children are asked to sing the notes they have written.

(c) For playing the chords they are asked to stand in line at the piano, and each child, in turn, to play the chords I V I in one of the successive keys as indicated in the circle of keys, and to continue until they have played the chords in all of the keys, and until rhythm and some speed have been acquired. The rhythm is maintained in this way:

(d) The same process is followed for connecting the I chord of the second and third positions with the nearest position of the V chord.

ILLUSTRATION

1. — 2nd position of the I chord.

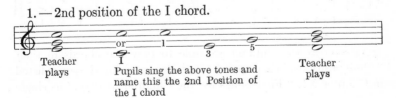

Teacher plays

Pupils sing the above tones and name this the 2nd Position of the I chord

Teacher plays

Pupils sing the above tones
and name this the 3rd Position of the V chord

Teacher
plays

Pupils sing

The children play in all of the successive keys:

I V I   I V I   I V I   I V I etc.

2. — 3rd Position of the I chord:—

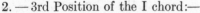

Teacher
plays

Pupils sing the above tones
and name this the 3rd Position of the I chord

Teacher plays

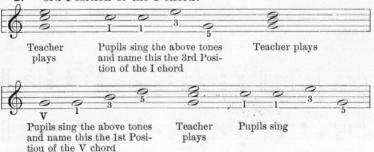

Pupils sing the above tones
and name this the 1st Posi-
tiou of the V chord

Teacher
plays

Pupils sing

The children play in all of the successive keys:—

I V I   I V I   I V I   I V I etc.

As soon as the children are able to play the chords in their
" close positions," they apply them in harmonizing the songs listed
in Chapter XI, " First Songs for the Children to Play," as single

chords on the first beat of each measure (in 4–4 time, the first and third beats), or, as chord accompaniments.

Illustrations of applying the chords in their " close positions " to the song, " Cuckoo," which is printed in 13 (*h*), this Chapter.

1. An accompaniment, as the song is sung:

Cuck-oo,   cuck-oo, Calls from the wood.   Let us be   sing-ing,

danc-ing and spring-ing, Spring-time,spring-time, Soon will be here.

(*e*) The same plan is followed for connecting the other Major and Minor chords of the scale, namely, the IV–ii–vi– and iii, after each has been separately introduced. The only rule necessary to apply in order that consecutive fifths and octaves shall not succeed each other, is never to connect two chords of the same *position*. The one exception, however, is the V₇ chord when connected with the V, since it is a continuation of the V.

The following are illustrations of " close positions " of the IV V₇ I chords. The others will be given in their regular order as introduced to the children.

2. — A single chord in each measure:

3. — A broken chord accompaniment:

4. — As jumping bass accompaniment:

The I chord in the first position connected in " close position " with the V and V₇ chords.

I V V₇ I I V V₇ I I V V₇ I etc.

The I chord in the second position connected in " close position " with the V and V₇ chords.

I V V₇ I I V V₇ I I V V₇ I etc.

The I chord in the third position connected in " close position " with the V and V₇ chords.

I V V₇ I I V V₇ I I V V₇ I etc.

Illustration of a Folk-Song harmonized with the I and V₇ Chords:

SPRINGTIME

German Folk-Tune

19. The IV or Subdominant Chord. This chord is frequently introduced, particularly to very small children, before the close positions of the I, V and V₇ chords, and before the " home-tone " of the V chord is sung above the keynote, in which case it is heard, sung and played in its most simple form, as,

It is assumed, however, that the preceding work in this chapter has been completed, in which case the children are prepared to sing the " home-tone " of the IV chord above the keynote (see Direction 15, present chapter) and to sing, write and play the chord in its three positions (as explained in Direction 17).

When a new chord is introduced, it is in connection with those that have preceded it, to give practice in maintaining scale and chord consciousness at the same time. The following directions and illustrations will exemplify this last idea.

DIRECTIONS

(a) The teacher plays the chords I, IV, V, V₇, I in many keys and asks the children to sing the root-tones of each.

(b) Songs listed in Chapter XI under " Songs that are Harmonized with the I, IV, V and V₇ Chords " are played and the children are asked to sing the chords they hear under each measure and to write the chord-patterns on the board.

(c) The chords are played for the children to sing and write the separate tones in many keys and to name the positions.

ILLUSTRATIONS

1st Position of the IV chord

2nd Position of the IV chord

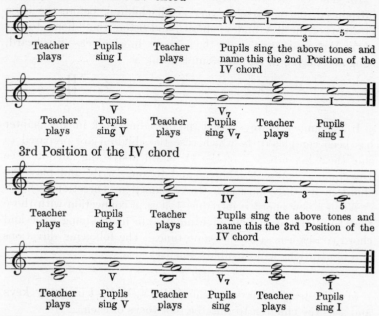

3rd Position of the IV chord

(d) The children are asked to play these chords as a chord-pattern in the three positions in all of the keys of the circle to the following rhythm, after which they are applied to the chord-patterns of the melodies.*

* As one child plays, the rest of the class sing the root tones.

20. The Minor Chords, II, VI and III. As an introduction to the Minor Mode, and to interest the children before the Minor scale is sung, Minor chords and Folk-songs and a Soldier Game are played, by means of which they will be able to recognize a Minor chord and melody. A review of this is advisable. See Chapter VII, " The Minor Scale."

(a) The separate tones of the Major and Minor Chords compared.

The teacher leads the children to discover that the only difference between a Major and a Minor chord is the third tone which is a " slide " or half-step below the Major. This is done by playing a Major and a Minor chord built on the same root, in the first position, in any key.

To hear this distinction clearly, they are asked to sing each separate tone and to name the distance by " slides " and " steps " between the first two tones of each chord. Between 1 and 3 of the Major, they will hear two " steps," and between the same numbers of the Minor, a " step " and a " slide." The teacher explains that the former is a *Major Interval* and the latter a Minor.

(b) A scale is written on the board, and it is shown that each tone, except the VII* (see note) is used for the root of a chord. The children are asked to write the chords by using each of these scale tones as a chord basis; to write the chord names under each, and to designate whether they are Major or Minor.

* The VII is omitted as a VII chord, since it is diminished; and diminished chords are reserved for a later study of harmony. At this time, it is explained as a continuation of the V chord which, with the root or "home-tone" of the V added makes it the V₇ with which the children are already familiar.

The following is the result:

The same general directions that have been given for the Major chords are now used for the development of the Minor. This is possible because the chord-spelling for both the Major and the Minor chords is the same — since the arrangement of the tones for each of the three positions is the same — and because a common rule applies for connecting the chords in their Close Positions.

So it has seemed necessary to give no more than the chord patterns and the three positions of the chords in the order in which they are presented to the children, together with the chords that have preceded them. These the teacher also introduces in connection with the songs listed in Chapter XI.

C — The II Chord (Super-tonic) for hearing, singing, and writing the 1st position of the II Chord.

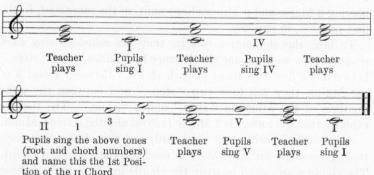

For hearing, singing, and writing the 2nd Position of the II Chord:

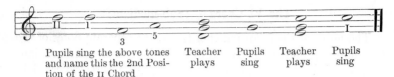

For hearing, singing, and writing the 3rd Position of the II Chord.

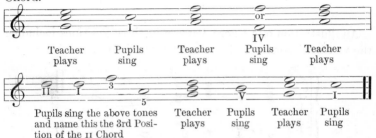

Illustration of a Chord Pattern in three Positions including the II Chord for the children to play in all keys.

The VI Chord — (Sub-mediant)

The notes of the following chords and the separate notes of the VI Chord are sung and written in many keys and their positions named as the teacher plays the chord phrase here indicated in its three positions, in a way that has been described and illustrated for the II Chord.

I   VI   II   V   I

An illustration of a Chord Pattern in three Positions including the VI Chord, for the children to play in all keys.

The III Chord — (Mediant)

The notes of the following chords and the separate notes of the III Chord are sung and written in many keys and the positions named as the teacher plays the chord-phrase here indicated in a way that has been illustrated for the II Chord.

I   III   IV   II   V   V₇   I

Illustration of a Chord Pattern in three Positions including the
III Chord, for the children to play in all keys.

MINOR KEYS

After the children are familiar with the Minor scales, the following chord pattern in its three positions is given to be played in all
the Minor keys, the chords of which are used for harmonization
for the Minor songs listed in Chapter XI under " A List of Songs
in Minor Keys."

The formation of the chords from a Minor scale:

CHORD PATTERN

A Minor:

CHAPTER XI

THE FIRST SONGS FOR THE CHILDREN TO PLAY

The songs listed in this chapter are given to the children as their first expression at the keyboard. The arrangement is such that they begin with the most simple Rhythm, Melody and Harmony, and progress stepwise so gradually that the children scarcely realize they are being led to something more difficult.

The chords are taken up in the order of their importance, and the melodies so chosen that the first selections are sung on the first two tones of the scale only, the next on the first three, and so on, until all of the tones above and below the "home-tone" have been used. The same simple plan has been followed, as nearly as possible, for the Rhythm.

The directions for developing the feeling for Rhythm (including Time and Phrasing) and the hearing of the " Melody " and " Harmony " have been described so explicitly under each separate subject in this volume, that a detailed description in the following directions is not given. A general plan, however, is offered for the teacher's use; and where this is not clear, reference should be made to the special subjects.

1. The teacher plays the song and the children sing and swing it. (The song " Swinging," is given as an illustration.)

Swinging

Swing-ing low, swing-ing high,Through the air we gai - ly fly.

2. The teacher plays it with expression and marked rhythm and phrasing while the children listen, name the complete and the incomplete phrases, and sing the " home-tone " whenever it occurs at the end of a complete phrase.

3. The children repeat the song by singing and swinging with a feeling of expression and rhythm.

4. They make " Pitch Pictures " with their hands of each phrase while singing.

5. They write the " Pitch Pictures " on the board — each phrase on a separate line, thus:

Swing - ing   low,   Swing - ing   high,

Through   the   air   we   gai - ly   fly.

6. They step the long and the short tones *while singing the song;* that is, the steps are held as long as the tones are held with the voice.

7. To the same long and short steps, they sing the *length of the tones* to the melody of the song, as:

" Short, short, long, short, short, long,
  Short, short, short, short, short, short, long."

8. They draw a " Duration Picture " on the board and in their blank music-books while singing the length of the tones to the melody of the song, like this:

<table>
<tr><td>short</td><td>short</td><td>long</td><td></td><td>short</td><td>short</td><td>long</td></tr>
<tr><td>short</td><td>short</td><td>short</td><td>short</td><td>short</td><td>short</td><td>long</td></tr>
</table>

9. They combine the " Pitch " and " Duration " pictures while singing the song, as:

Swing - ing low, Swing - ing high,

Through the air we gai - ly fly.

For Adding the Bar Lines

10. They sing and swing the song to feel particularly, the place where each swing changes. Then (while singing the words), they swing with their left hands and draw the bar lines with their right, at the places in the " Pitch " and " Duration " picture where each swing begins and ends. At the beginning and end of the song, they draw double bar lines.

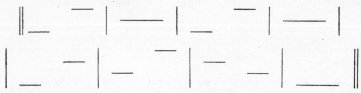

11. They add the stems to the " Pitch " and " Duration " lines while singing the words of the song.

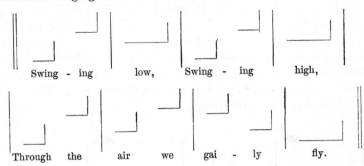

12. The teacher tells the children that " short " means a quarter note and " long " a half note (see Chapter IV, Rhythmic Notation). The children step again and sing the note values to the melody, thus:

Quarter, quarter, half, — quarter, quarter, half —
Quarter, quarter, quarter, quarter, quarter, quarter, half.

13. They add the note values to the " Duration and Pitch " pictures while singing them to the tune of the song. Example:

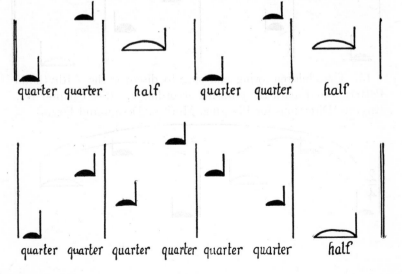

14. The teacher plays the song for the children to clap the Time in order to discover the Time-signature. (For this the directions are given in Chapter III, Rhythm — for singing Rhythm and Clapping Time.) When all agree as to the number of beats in each measure, they are asked to clap and sing and compare the number of claps given to each note indicated on the " Pitch and Duration " picture that they may discover for themselves that a quarter note is given one clap and a half-note, two. They add the Time-signature agreed upon.

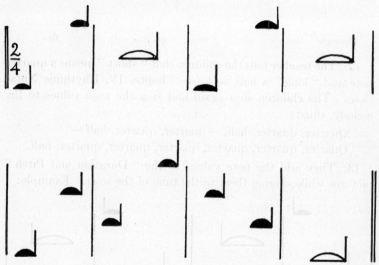

15. The children swing and sing to discover the " Rhythmic Pattern " and mark the phrasing accordingly. (See Chapter III, Rhythm Directions for Phrasing, Motif or Design and Form.)

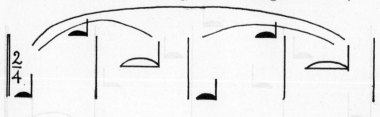

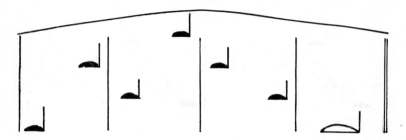

NOTE. — In this song, as the "Rhythmic Phrase" begins on the first beat of the measure and ends on the last, the most simple "Rhythmic Pattern" is illustrated.

16. For translating the " Pitch Pictures " tones into the scale tone numbers, or, for hearing definitely the steps, slides and leaps, the teacher uses any of the games or drills in Chapter VIII, Melody. They write these numbers or steps, slides and leaps, as they sing them above the " Pitch " and " Duration Pattern."

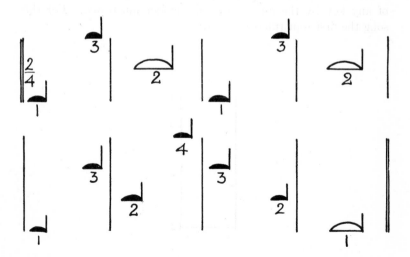

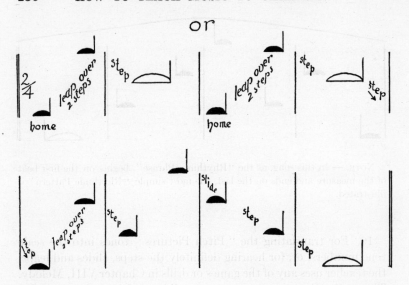

17. They change the numbers of the above into the letter names of any key by the use of the scale ladder illustrated. For this song the first four rungs are used:

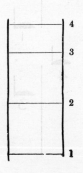

and the " home-tone " is changed to represent the key-note or
" home-tone " of any of the twelve keys, as:

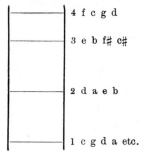

4 f c g d

3 e b f♯ c♯

2 d a e b

1 c g d a etc.

The children sing the letters to the melody of the song as they
write them.

18. It may be possible, at this time, for the children to write
the notes of the song immediately in their blank music-books, in
any key, without assistance of the teacher or of the keyboard;
but if not, the directions for " Melodic Dictation, Chapter IX,
Notation," are followed.

19. They add the Bar lines, Time signature, Note values, and
Phrase lines by referring, if necessary, to the completed " Rhythmic Pattern," No. 15, in this chapter.

20. They write the song in several keys.

21. While singing and pretending to play in the air, each child
decides for himself the fingering that will connect the tones of each
phrase smoothly.

22. The teacher asks each child, in turn, to go to the keyboard
and to play a scale in a given key; then to play the song in that
key just as it was sung or felt; or, in other words, to listen as the
tones are made to sing the song or tell the story. (See Chapter
XII, Technique.)

23. The teacher plays the song as the children sing the chords
that harmonize with each measure, and, while doing so, write a
chord pattern on the board, as:

‖ I | V | I | V |

| I | V | V | I ‖

24. Each child plays the chords in different keys as the class sings the song.

25. Each child, in turn, harmonizes the melody in a different key. (For details in Harmonization see Chapter X, Harmony, and Melodic and Harmonic Dictation in Chapter IX, Notation.)

A LIST OF THE FIRST SONGS FOR THE CHILDREN TO PLAY

The songs in the following list will be found complete in the supplement to this volume, " The Children's Own Book."

The songs are arranged in groups according to the number of scale-tones used (*) and are graded gradually from the simplest Rhythm, note-values and Harmonization, to the more complex.

SONGS IN MAJOR KEYS

To be Harmonized with the I and V or V₇ Chords

†1. Come and Sing a Song to Me.
2. Far Away the Robin Sings.
3. Little Blue Pigeon.
4. Sunshine Bright.
5. Pat-a-Cake.
6. Lullaby.
7. Hot Cross Buns.
8. Swinging.
9. Bye-lo Dolly Dear.
10. Wee Son John.
11. Springtime.
12. Cuckoo.
13. The Nightingale.
14. Bye-Baby, Bye.
15. Hum, Hum, Hum.
16. Make Hay by the Neckar.
17. Hymn of Praise.

* The number of scale tones used for each group of songs is indicated in the supplement.
† As the list is not arranged alphabetically, the songs may be more readily found in "The Children's Own Book," by giving number as well as title.

18. Fais Dodo.
19. A Rooster and a Gander.
20. Pretty Little Hildegarde
21. Le Petit Chasseur.
22. Dancing Fairies.
23. English Folk Dance.
24. The Rhine Motive.
25. Where Are You Going?
26. The Robin's Song.
27. Savez-vous Planter les Choux?
28. Bugle Call.
29. The May Queen.
30. Hop, Hop, Hop.
31. A Fairy Game.
32. Looby Loo.
33. Ah! Mon beau Chateau.
34. Le Pont d'Avignon.
35. As-tu vu la Casquette?
36. Frère Jacques.
37. Come Let Us Be Dancing.
38. Lieber Augustin.

To be Harmonized with the I, IV and V or V₇ Chords

39. Lavender's Blue.
40. Ah! Vous Dirai-je-Maman.
41. Cradle Song.
42. In the Blue and Silver Sky.
43. Round and Round the Village.
44. I had a Little Nut-Tree.
45. Spring is Here!
46. There Came to My Window.
47. La Bonne Aventure.
48. The Silver Moon.
49. Little Jack Horner.
50. A Frog He Would a-Wooing Go.
51. Silent Night.
52. The Elf-man (Jack-in-the-Pulpit).
53. Swedish Folk-dance.

To be Harmonized with the I, IV, V or V₇ and II Chords

54. Come and Dance on the Hillside.
55. Sailing and Flying.
56. The Dancing Pig.
57. The Air-ship.
58. Au Clair de la Lune.
59. Yankee Doodle.
60. The Hunter's Horn.
61. How Many Miles to Boston Town?
62. Oh Mountain Pine.
63. Hippity Hop.
64. Oh! Dear What Can the Matter Be?
65. Little Jumping Joan.
66. The Blue-bird.
67. Snow-capped Mountains.

To be Harmonized with the I, IV, II, VI and V or V₇ Chords

68. Cock-a-doo-dle-doo.
69. Racing Leaves.
70. America.
71. The Crested Hen.
72. The Little Dustman.
73. Curly Locks.
74. Hey, Diddle, Diddle.
75. I Saw a Ship a-Sailing
76. The Buzzard.

To be Harmonized with the I, IV, II, VI, III and V or V₇ Chords

77. The Crooked Man.
78. Lott ist Tod.
79. Gaily the Troubadour.
80. St. Patrick's Day.

SONGS IN MINOR KEYS

To be Harmonized with the I and V or V₇ Chords

81. The Reindeer.
82. The Old Chateau.

To be Harmonized with the I, IV and V or V₇ Chords

83. London Town.
84. Slavonic Folk Tune.
85. Dame Get Up and Bake Your Pies.
86. The Evening Star.

To be Harmonized with the I, IV, II and V or V₇ Chords

87. The North-Wind.
88. Summer is Gone.

To be Harmonized with the I, IV, VI and V or V₇ Chords

89. Old King Cole

CHAPTER XII

TECHNIQUE

It is impossible to stress too earnestly the importance of never *sending a child to the piano to practice:* the instrument is to be sought only when the need is felt to play upon it the songs and selections that the child has been hearing. He thus goes to the piano in the creative spirit of play; and as the psychology of creative playing is the native impulse of the child, he is caught joyfully in the work by the law of life itself.

Parents should be given the key to this situation and so relieved from their old anxiety as to the need of regular practicing hours for children. In fact, the teacher should be in close understanding with the parents upon this fundamental principle. It must be understood that the process is slow; that the results are not immediate; in short, the parent must be converted to an idea of what *not* to expect from the child in the beginning. These anxious ones must be persuaded to wait upon a slower and later growth of the child's interest, when he will be awakened and his musical consciousness so developed that the piano will be sought voluntarily for the pure joy of interpretation and self-expression.

For musical expression in class work, very little technique is advisable. The children learn relaxation from hearing and play as they feel.

Before they go to the keyboard, the teacher should lead them to understand that the piano is never to be touched except to "make music"; that every sound is to mean something, and that they are to listen as their fingers drop, and decide for themselves whether they are giving the tones the same meaning or feeling they expressed while singing. That when they play, they are to feel the same rhythmic swing that impelled them to move their arms and bodies as the songs were heard and sung; that is, to feel each phrase to the end and to realize that each tone is but a part of the whole, which is moving forward toward some definite goal. When combined with the melodic and harmonic knowledge previously acquired, the results of this process will be *relaxation* and *complete concentration*. If there is an inclination on the part of the pupils to play too rapidly, the teacher asks them to listen for the echo of each tone. This often helps to give freedom and repose at the keyboard.

When a child is given private lessons (see Chapter I, " When Private Lessons should Begin ") the technical problem is dealt with more specifically. But before any technical study is attempted, it is incumbent upon the teacher to have already created such an interest on the part of the pupils that they will be most eager and willing to devote any needed time and energy in obtaining the desired results.

It is also essential that the teacher herself be equipped with such thorough and fundamental technical ability that she may intelligently meet and overcome all difficulties which will naturally arise as the musical education of the pupil progresses. Helpful books on this subject are:

MATTHAY, TOBIAS AUGUSTUS. The Act of Touch in all its diversity, *Longmans, N. Y.*
MASON, WILLIAM. Touch and Technique for Artistic Piano Playing, *Presser, Philadelphia.*

CHAPTER XIII

THE MUSICAL STORY PERIOD

"The course of life goes on in one increasing flow from beginning to end. If we wish our pupils to be artists, we must begin our development of the instinct for art, at the commencement of our teaching and continue it through the whole course of musical education." — T. H. YORKE TROTTER.

"To train the perceptive faculties by means of which man lays hold upon the world that surrounds him, and draws it into himself, and makes it his own, is the highest achievement of the teacher's art." — EDMOND HOLMES.

There is no more effective means of developing the instinct for art, which is latent in every normal child, than by the use of stories illustrated with music. Children love them and beg for them. They have proven to be among the most potent factors in education. They enlarge the consciousness, awaken the imagination, and give the child the needed material for creating his own dream-world, which is a source of never-ending delight. The ideals and images formed at this time, become a treasure-house for later use when the creative urge and musical development have grown to such proportions that self-expression becomes a real necessity. From the vast domain of music, the teacher draws upon unfailing stores of enchanting lore which remain an open sesame of inspiration for both young and old. Indeed, this realm of story-telling is a veritable fairy land for the imaginative child; and it is every child's right to dwell therein.

The subjects are chosen from the Evolution or History of Music (as referred to in Chapter IX, Notation); from Musical Folklore; from the lives of the composers — particularly the events that are associated with their childhood and the incidents that have inspired their best known compositions; and from the ideas expressed in the famous symphonies, sonatas and operas, such as, Wagner's "Niebelungen Lied," "Parsifal"; also Humperdinck's "Hänsel and Gretel," etc.

For material, the teacher should consult the Reference Rooms — both the Children's and Adults' Departments — of the best Musical Libraries.

The following is a short list of books for the teacher to own:

KOBBE, GUSTAVE. Wagner's Music Dramas, analyzed with the leading motives, *Schirmer, N. Y.*

LAVIGNAC, ALBERT. Musical Dramas of Richard Wagner, *Nisbet, London.*

LILLIE, LUCY C. Story of Music and Musicians, *Harper, N. Y.*

PARRY, SIR CHAS., HUBERT, HASTINGS. Johann Sebastian Bach, *Putnam, N. Y.*

PERRY, EDWARD B. Stories of Standard Teaching Pieces, *Presser Co., Philadelphia.*

SMITH, HANNAH. Founders of Music, *Schirmer, N. Y.*

TAPPER, THOMAS. First Studies in Musical Biography, *Presser Co., Philadelphia.*

HUBBARD, ELBERT. Little Journeys to the Homes of Great Composers, *Putnam, N. Y.*

RIPLEY, F. H. AND SCHNEIDER, E. The Art-Music Readers, Books I and II, *Atkinson, Mentzer & Co., New York.*

Every story should be illustrated with music in order to give the children the meaning of the music that words will convey and guide them in realizing that this meaning is deeper than even language can express; in short, to aid them in learning the language of music.

With the stories of the Operas, Symphonies and Sonatas, motives may be played for the children to sing (they are later used for expression in all keys for class-work); at which time the teacher may play the compositions in their entirety.

Motives may be secured directly from the musical scores, but a few have been found to be published. They are:

Motives from Symphonies

BEETHOVEN. Fifth Symphony, First Movement, Main Theme; Second Movement, Andante *con moto.* In Progressive Music Series, Teacher's Manual, Vol. IV, p. 171.

HAYDN. Symphony in G, First and Second Movements, Progressive Music Series, Teacher's Manual, Vol. IV, p. 102.

MOZART. Symphony in E♭, First and Second Movements, Progressive Music Series, Teacher's Manual, Vol. IV, p. 9.

Motives from Sonatas

BEETHOVEN. Sonata, Appassionata, First Movement, Main Theme, Progressive Music Series, Teacher's Manual, Vol. IV, p. 67.

BEETHOVEN. Moonlight Sonata, First and Second Movements, Progressive Music Series, Teacher's Manual, Vol. IV, p. 17.

BEETHOVEN. Sonata Pathétique, First Movement, Introduction Theme; First Movement, Main Theme, Progressive Music Series, Teacher's Manual, Vol. IV, p. 58.

Motives from Operas

WAGNER. The Rhinegold, The Valkyr, Siegfried, The Dusk of the Gods, Parsifal, In KOBBÉ, GUSTAV, Wagner's Music Dramas, analyzed with the leading motives, *Schirmer, N. Y.*

About five or ten minutes may be reserved at the end of each class-lesson for the story period, and the musical selections given are repeated many times, that the children may become so familiar with them that they will be instantly recognized by melody and name. When a preference has been formed, they are given the privilege of asking for them, if time permits, to which request the teacher always responds.

CHILDREN'S MUSICAL PARTIES

(As They are Called by Mrs. Seymour)

Musical Parties are original and novel and a source of joy and inspiration to the children. They may be given monthly or bi-monthly on Saturday afternoons when the different groups of all the classes are brought together to be entertained. The teacher does this by giving a program that is prepared to catch and hold their interest and at the same time prove instructive

The Musical Parties follow the same plan of story and music as given at the end of each class-lesson, except that there is sufficient time for programs of greater length. These afternoons are happy events in the lives of the children.

For a season's program, it is advisable to choose the subjects within a certain period of time, arrange them in chronological order, giving to each composer an afternoon, and to occasionally vary these outlines with a mixed program.

As the teacher entertains, she must intuitively know when to continue or end her stories and music, as the object is to maintain the keenest interest throughout the unique hour. The author wishes at this point to earnestly warn teachers of the great danger of talking too much. Their stories, descriptions and explanations should be brief and to the point.

When she finishes her part — which is at a time when the interest is still at its height — she tells the children that the program will be prolonged if any of them will volunteer to play. In no instance will this invitation fail, if properly introduced; for after one or two children have responded, all are eager to contribute, and the usual difficulty is to end the " party " within a reasonable time.

Should there be indications of self-consciousness — which scarcely seems possible, owing to the freedom obtained in the classes — it could be overcome by the singing of class songs and the playing of singing games.

When the children respond by their own volition and without preparation, fear is eliminated; they are eager to participate, and they play with freedom and without a trace of stage-fright.

To serve as a typical illustration, the following is a program of a Children's Party at the Seymour School.

1. Story and music from the " Niebelungen " Lied by Wagner.
The story of Brünhilde and Siegfried was told and the leading motives given at the time reference was made to them, after which the Slumber, Fire and Siegfried music was played.

2. Story: An event in Schumann's life and something of his compositions for children.
Music: " The Wild Horseman."
Romance: " The Merry Farmer."

3. Story: A short narrative of Bach's family life and of the compositions written for his children.
Music: Minuet in G.

4. Story: Mozart's and Beethoven's lives and habits of writing compared.
From the description given, the children were asked to listen attentively to a minuet by Beethoven and another by Mozart, and, at the end, to be able to decide upon the composer of each.
The minuets played were:
    Beethoven's in G minor.
    Mozart's from Don Giovanni.

5. A short story of Chopin's life, including his habits and manner of composing while living in an old monastery on the Island of Majorca.

Music: Prelude in A major.

6. An event in Gluck's life.

The story and music of his composition " Iphigenia."

7. Stories to describe the differences between " banging " and interpretative playing. Folk-dances were used for both and the children asked which they preferred. The dances played were:

Irish, Scotch, English and Bohemian from Burchenal and Crampton's Folk-dance Music.

Thus through simple fundamentals, the teacher is given a definite means of working according to a principle.

Music being a symbol of life, these fundamentals lead not only to an inner realization followed by an outer harmonious expression in music, but to the consciousness of a hidden power which safely guides us through existence.

THE END